CAMBRIDGE LIBRARY COLLECTION

Books of enduring scholarly value

Printing and publishing history

The interface between authors and their readers is a fascinating subject in its own right, revealing a great deal about social attitudes, technological progress, aesthetic values, fashionable interests, political positions, economic constraints, and individual personalities. This part of the Cambridge Library Collection reissues classic studies in the area of printing and publishing history that shed light on developments in typography and book design, printing and binding, the rise and fall of publishing houses and periodicals, and the roles of authors and illustrators. It documents the ebb and flow of the book trade supplying a wide range of customers with products from almanacs to novels, bibles to erotica, and poetry to statistics.

Historical Account of the Substances Which have been Used to Describe Events, and to Convey Ideas, from the Earliest Date, to the Invention of Paper

Matthias Koops was a pioneer of mechanical paper-making. He invented new processes for making paper from wood pulp rather than from rags, and for recycling paper itself to a condition in which it could be used for printing. The first edition (1800) of this book was printed entirely on paper which he had produced from straw, but the paper has darkened over the years, making reproduction difficult. The second edition of 1801, dedicated like the first to King George III, was printed partly on a better type of straw paper and partly on recycled paper; the Appendix was 'printed on paper made from wood alone, the produce of this country, without any intermixture of rags, waste paper, bark, straw, or any other vegetable substance'. Koops's aim was to overcome the problem of the scarcity of rags for paper-making, which he believed was a restraint on the development of commerce and of science, by producing paper from natural sources which were almost inexhaustible. However, the factory which he established for manufacturing his papers went bankrupt after only one year, and it was to be nearly two centuries before his ambition to print new books on paper made from recycled old ones became a practical possibility for the industry.

Cambridge University Press has long been a pioneer in the reissuing of out-of-print titles from its own backlist, producing digital reprints of books that are still sought after by scholars and students but could not be reprinted economically using traditional technology. The Cambridge Library Collection extends this activity to a wider range of books which are still of importance to researchers and professionals, either for the source material they contain, or as landmarks in the history of their academic discipline.

Drawing from the world-renowned collections in the Cambridge University Library, and guided by the advice of experts in each subject area, Cambridge University Press is using state-of-the-art scanning machines in its own Printing House to capture the content of each book selected for inclusion. The files are processed to give a consistently clear, crisp image, and the books finished to the high quality standard for which the Press is recognised around the world. The latest print-on-demand technology ensures that the books will remain available indefinitely, and that orders for single or multiple copies can quickly be supplied.

The Cambridge Library Collection will bring back to life books of enduring scholarly value (including out-of-copyright works originally issued by other publishers) across a wide range of disciplines in the humanities and social sciences and in science and technology.

Historical Account of the Substances Which have been Used to Describe Events, and to Convey Ideas, from the Earliest Date, to the Invention of Paper

Matthias Koops

CAMBRIDGE
UNIVERSITY PRESS

CAMBRIDGE UNIVERSITY PRESS

Cambridge, New York, Melbourne, Madrid, Cape Town, Singapore,
São Paolo, Delhi, Dubai, Tokyo

Published in the United States of America by Cambridge University Press, New York

www.cambridge.org
Information on this title: www.cambridge.org/9781108009041

© in this compilation Cambridge University Press 2009

This edition first published 1801
This digitally printed version 2009

ISBN 978-1-108-00904-1 Paperback

The Egyptian Papyrus, or Paper Rush;
Taken from Prosper Alpinus.

HISTORICAL ACCOUNT

OF THE

SUBSTANCES

WHICH HAVE BEEN USED TO

DESCRIBE EVENTS, AND TO CONVEY IDEAS,

FROM THE

EARLIEST DATE

TO THE

INVENTION OF PAPER.

SECOND EDITION.

PRINTED ON PAPER RE-MADE FROM OLD PRINTED AND
WRITTEN PAPER.

By *MATTHIAS KOOPS, Esq.*

LONDON:

PRINTED BY JAQUES AND CO. 30, LOWER SLOANE STREET.
1801.

TO

HIS MOST EXCELLENT MAJESTY

𝕲𝕰𝕺𝕽𝕲𝕰 𝕿𝕳𝕰 𝕿𝕳𝕴𝕽𝕯,

KING

OF

THE UNITED KINGDOMS

OF

GREAT-BRITAIN

AND

IRELAND.

MOST GRACIOUS SOVEREIGN.

SIRE,

YOUR MAJESTY having been Moſt Grac:ouſly pleaſed to grant me Patents for extracting printing and writing ink from waſte Paper, by reducing it to a pulp, and converting it into *white Paper*, fit for writing, printing, and for other purpoſes; and alſo for manufacturing Paper from Straw, Hay, Thiſtles, waſte and refuſe of Hemp and Flax, and different kinds of Wood and Bark, fit for printing, and almoſt all other purpoſes for which Paper is uſed,

And

And YOUR MAJESTY having in September laſt year condeſcended to permit me to lay at Your feet the firſt uſeful Paper which has ever been made from Straw alone* without any addition of rags; the Gracious Reception it has met with from YOUR MAJESTY, the approbation of the Publick, and the encouragement which the Legiſlature has given me by paſſing an Act of Parliament in its favour has engaged me to reprint theſe lines on Paper manufactured from Straw ſolely in a more improved ſtate, although not yet brought to ſuch a ſtate of perfection as it will be made in a regular manufacture, which muſt be entirely

* Part of this Edition is printed on Straw Paper.

conſtructed

conftructed for fuch purpofe, and which I moft humbly flatter myfelf will now much fooner be eftablifhed by the indulgence which YOUR MAJESTY's Parliament has granted me. This new Effay proves, there cannot be any doubt that good and ufeful Paper can be made from Straw alone.

The favourable manner in which YOUR MAJESTY has deigned to look on thefe my humble attempts of dif-covery fhall be a conftant incitement to future exertions, and the profpect of meriting commendation of a KING, always ready to countenance the moft humble endeavours which tend to the common welfare, and who has proved

Himfelf

Himself the Illuftrious Patron and Protector of Arts and Sciences, obliges me to unremitted perfeverance to bring my attempts to perfection, in the profpect of meriting YOUR MAJESTY's commendation, which will be the greateft pleafure I can be fenfible of.

With the moft ardent wifhes for YOUR MAJESTY's health and longevity, and with all poffible deference and humility, I beg leave, MOST GRACIOUS SOVEREIGN, to fubfcribe myfelf,

YOUR MAJESTY's

moft devoted,

moft obedient,

and moft humble Servant,

17, James-ftreet.
Buckingham-gate,
Auguft 30, 1801.

MATTHIAS KOOPS.

THE art of Paper-making ought to be regarded as one of the moſt uſeful which has ever been invented in **any age** or country; for it is manifeſt, that every other diſcovery muſt have continued uſelefs **to** ſociety if it could not have been diffeminated by manuſcripts, or by printing.

Scientific men, who were neither artiſts nor manufacturers, have, by means of this invention, been enabled to communicate their projects, which mechanics have afterwards improved and perfected, and by this means enriched the commonwealth.

Without

Without the ufe of Paper, geography and navigation muft have been very incorrectly underftood; the beautiful charts of the ocean fo accurately laid down have eftablifhed our commercial intercourfe with every part of the globe with fafety; at the fame time that the delineations upon maps of places, rivers, and countries, are now fo correct, that they enable a traveller to proceed without danger, and even predict, with certainty, the time it will require to convey him to any part of the globe.

It may be afferted, indeed, of this country, that its grandeur and commercial dignity have been greatly exalted by the invention of Paper; for it is prefumed, that the fuperiority which diftinguifhes the manufactures of this Ifland, chiefly depends upon the liberal publications concentered from all the reft of the world, which have fo greatly increafed in latter years, and which are likely

farther

farther to be augmented. It is, in fhort, the reputation of the goods fabricated in Great-Britain, which has elevated it to the fplendour and fame it now poffeffes, in the fcale of nations, and enables it to monopolize the trade of the uni-verfe.—All thefe are benefits which have flowed from the invention of Paper, and which have fo largely contributed to the prefent flourifhing ftate of the country.

What infinite trouble and labour, what a fruitlefs confumption of time has not been faved by the knowledge of Paper! how many laborious and dangerous ex-periments have not philofophical projec-tors been fpared! what labour of invef-tigation and ftudy have not been abridged by the events which the experiments of others have handed down to pofterity! thereby affording to the prefent age a body of information more than adequate to the knowledge any one man could

have

have attained to, in a thoufand years, with all his faculties.

This reflection alone, muſt fix fuch an impreſſion on any thinking mind of the invaluable utility of Paper, as to render any further commendation unneceſſary; but in ſhort, the inventions of Paper and Printing have been the cauſes of the various gradations of improvement in every art and ſcience. Without it, the preſent age would neither have been more civilized nor wiſer than it was many centuries ago, becauſe one age could never have conveyed to its poſterity, what the labours of the paſt had atchieved; for it is well known, that, in dark and barbarous ages, the inhabitants of no country have ever made any progreſs towards improvement and civilization, with-out the uſe of Writing, Printing, and Paper; and it ſeems very probable, that the early knowledge of this article amongſt the Chineſe, has been the cauſe of thoſe

acquire-

acquirements which have diftinguifhed that truly wonderful nation: for it may be affirmed, that in proportion to the quantity of Paper confumed, by any ftated number of inhabitants in literary purfuits, fo will be their comparative information, civilized ftate, and improvement.

To enumerate all the various advantages which the invention of Paper has afforded mankind, could not be contained in an Effay of this nature: its ufes are unqueftionable; and the important fervices it has yielded to all countries where it has been employed are not to be calculated; it is fufficient to fay here, that the growing youth are educated with facility in the principles of their duty, and barbarous ftates have been foftened and enlightened by means of this difcovery.

Although this fubject might be much enlarged upon, the intention of this Addrefs is moft humbly to prefent to *Your*

Moft

Moſt Gracious Majeſty the *firſt* uſeful Paper manufactured *ſolely* from *Straw*, and on which theſe lines are printed. *

From the remarks which have been already made, every perſon muſt be convinced, that it is of the utmoſt conſequence to prevent a ſcarcity of the materials from which Paper is to be fabricated. Although cotton has been likewiſe uſed for this purpoſe, paper-makers in this country have depended on linen Rags for the regular purſuit of their employment.

All Europe has of late years experienced, an extraordinary ſcarcity of this article, but no country has been ſo much injured by it as England. The greatly advanced price, and the abſolute ſcarcity, equally operating to obſtruct many printing-preſſes in this kingdom; and various works remain, for theſe reaſons, unpubliſhed, which

* Part of this edition is printed on remanufactured white Paper.

might

might have proved very ferviceable to the community.

The great demands for Paper in this country have rendered it neceffary to fupply its mills from the continent with Rags. This fupply is extremely precarious, and is likely to be more wanted, as the con-fumption of Paper increafes, becaufe this material, which is the bafis of Paper, is not to be obtained in England in fufficient quantity. The evil confequence of not having a due fupply of Rags has been the ftoppage of a number of Paper-mills; and as it is a manufactory which requires numerous hands (of men, women, and children); a great number of them have been thrown upon their refpective parifhes for want of employment. A ftill more important confideration, in the view of commerce, prefents itfelf, when the raw material comes from abroad, becaufe the importation of it is paid in hard cafh,

the

the preparation of which might have advantageoufly employed numbers of idle hands at home.

Thefe reflections induced me to make various experiments, with a view to remedy, in fome degree, this evil; and, after many trials, I have the fatisfaction to remark, that I have difcovered feveral fubftitutes for linen Rags, which have been heretofore unknown, or the experiments unfuccefsful, and which will merit the attention of the public. One of thefe difcoveries is the Art of extracting Printing and Writing Ink from Wafte Paper, whether in fmall or large pieces, by obliterating the ink, and rendering the Paper perfectly white, *without injuring the texture* of the regenerated Paper, and of a quality as good as it originally was, for the purpofes of writing and re-printing.

It is worthy of the directors of families to order their fervants to fave all the wafte

White

White Paper, fuch as letters and old writing-paper, which are generally thrown away or burnt, and regarded as of no confequence; for, fhould this be attended to, very confiderable quantities would be collected, and large fums of money faved, which are now expended in foreign countries for Rags; becaufe, if we calculate that Great Britain contains fifteen hundred thoufand families, and that half a fheet of Paper fhould be daily faved in every family, it would produce four thoufand four hundred tons,* which is about one-third of the quantity of Rags which have, of late, been converted annually into Paper in this country, whereby near two hundred thoufand pounds would annually remain in this country, which fum is now fent abroad for the purchafe of Rags; and eighty-two thoufand one hundred and twenty-five pounds would be faved from fire

* A ream, or five hundred fheets, being calculated at eighteen pounds weight.

fire and deftruction, calculating a pound of old Paper torn into pieces at two pence.

It has been imagined, that the prefent war has principally contributed to produce the fcarcity of Paper-ftuff, which, however, does not appear to be the fole caufe, becaufe the quantity of Rags ufed for making lint is very inconfiderable, compared to the enormous quantity at prefent ufed for the manufacture of Paper. Cartridges have ufually been made on the continent of old written Paper, which heretofore has been of no other ufe to Paper-makers than for the fabrication of pafte-boards.—It appears, from various confiderations, that the fcarcity has originated from the extenfion of learning, which occafions much larger quantities of Paper for writing and printing; the large increafe of newfpapers and monthly publications. Additional ftationers, printers, and bookfellers, countenance this opinion.

opinion. More children are now every where taught to read and write; and the hand-bills of every defcription, ufed for fhopkeepers, plays, quackery, and other trades, require additional quantities of Paper. Paper-hanging, which is an in-vention of the middle of the feventeenth century, has, of late years, become more general; and few new-built houfes are finifhed with walls, or wainfcot, as for-merly, but the furface is every where decorated with painted or ftained Paper, which is the moft beautiful, the cleaneft, and the cheapeft ornament for furnifhing rooms.

I beg leave to obferve, that little general knowledge, upon this ufeful fubject, has been hitherto communicated to the public; I, therefore, will endeavour to give a brief hiftorical account of the various methods and materials which have been ufed to convey ideas to pofterity, from the moft
ancient

ancient date to the period when the art of
making Paper, from linen rags, was invented.

The art of writing, in itfelf, proves that
mankind, at the time of its invention,
muft already have been in a certain degree civilized, and cannot therefore be
very ancient; but the exact time when
this art was difcovered is impoffible to
be traced.

The invention of *letters*, and their various
combinations, in the forming of words in
any language, has fomething fo ingenious
and *wonderful* in it, that moft who have
treated thereof, can hardly forbear attri-
buting it to a *divine original*, and fpeaking
of it with fuch a high admiration which
is not far from a kind of rapture. Indeed,
if we confider of what vaft, and even daily
fervice it is to mankind, it muft be certainly
allowed to be one of the *greateft*, and moft

furprizing

furprizing difcoveries that ever was made in the world. No perfon can deny of what general ufe the art of writing is in commerce; in contracts of every kind; in preferving, improving, and propagating learning and knowledge; in communicating our fentiments to, and correfponding with our friends, with thofe we love, or others, at any diftance, whither letters can be conveyed. And by the means of writing, as the moft valuable of all its advantages, we have a code of divine laws, ufeful hiftory, indifputable revelations, as a conftant *directory* for our conduct, in our courfe through this probationary ftate of life, to a happy eternity.

Notwithftanding thefe great and manifold benefits, which men have all along received from this curious and wonderful invention, it is very remarkable, that writing, which gives fome degree of *immortality*

tality to almoſt all other things, ſhould be, by the diſpoſal of Divine Providence, ſo ordered, as to be careleſs in preſerving the memory of its firſt founders. No archives are preſerved, wherein the names of thoſe perſons are repoſited, that have deſerved ſo much of mankind, by inventing the *characters*, and *alphabets*, proper to expreſs their own language and thoughts! If we enquire only after our own country way of writing, who can tell us the names of thoſe ingenious men, that firſt found out the *alphabets* uſed in our offices of records, or indeed any hand in uſe amongſt us?

Some make objections to this boaſted *utility* of writing, and likewiſe to the new-diſcovered ſubſtitutes for Paper-ſtuff, by which the quantity of Paper, unavoidably neceſſary for writing, will be ſo greatly encreaſed. They alledge, that the

the *inconveniencies*, and *evils*,* that letters
are the caufes of, are equal to, if not
more, than the *advantages* that arife therefrom. *Vicious* and *libertine* books, fay
they, are the lafting fources of corruption
in *faith* and *morals*. By the means of
Paper and writing, falfe notions in religion,
and even highly irritating herefies are
broached, and fpeedily propagated; trai-
torous correfpondencies are held, and de-
ceitful contrivances are carried on to the
ruin of private families, and often to the
deftruction of happinefs in wedlock; and
fometimes to the fubverfion of public ad-
miniftrations and government, which we

* *N. Tate*, Poet Laureat in Queen *Anne*'s time,
wrote the following lines on the *good* and *evil* of
writing.

> View writing's art, that like a fovereign Queen
> Amongft her fubjects fciences are feen ;
> As fhe in dignity the reft tranfcends,
> So far her power of good and harm extends ;
> And ftrange effects in both from her we find,
> The *Pallas* and *Pandora* of mankind.

have

have in late years experienced in the major part of Europe.—It is certain that much mifchief has arifen from Paper and Writing; and yet what is it but faying, that the pen is as dangerous an inftrument in the world as the tongue? muft we therefore renounce the ufe of the one, as well as the other? This would be a fanatical extreme, that all perfons of common fenfe and common prudence will avoid and abhor: for it is evident, that it is not the proper ufe, but the abufe of the art, that is objected againft.

Lycurgus, a king of *Thrace*, obferving the bad effects of wine amongft fuch of his fubjects who drank it to excefs, had all the vines in his kingdom cut down and deftroyed. Can any one applaud that king's contrivance, as a piece of wifdom? or was it not rather a foolifh and frantic act? The fame muft be applied to the above fubject; for as there is hardly any

one

one ufeful and good thing in the world but
what may be perverted to bad purpofes;
fo the abufe of Paper and Writing is a
poor argument againft the general and
great utility thereof. There have been
fome perfons like *Lycurgus*, of *Thrace*,
of this erroneous way of reafoning, with
regard to letters; *Thamus*, an ancient
Egyptian king, as is ftated in *Plato's Phæ-
drus*, remonftrated againft the ufe thereof;
as alfo againft the reception of the ufeful
parts of the mathematics, when *Theut*
offered to introduce them amongft his
fubjects. *Licinius*, a *Roman* emperor likewife, was a great enemy to letters, and
ufed men of learning and philofophers
with outrageous cruelty, calling them *the
bane and peft of fociety.* But thefe muft
be looked upon as the extravagant notions and whims of ignorant perfons who
obftinately glory to deviate from common
fenfe and the judgment of mankind; and
therefore ought to be no further regarded,

c   than

than for their fingularity, and the abfurd confequences that attend them.

Another pretext againft the ufe of Paper and Writing feems to be more plaufible than the former is, that it is an encouragement to a lazy difpofition. The objector fays, if we truft too much to books, or only write out what we ought to commit to our memories, we may in that be faid to lean to a broken ftaff; and be apt to imagine ourfelves more learned and knowing than in reality we are. It is not the poffeffion of an extenfive and beautiful library with learned books that makes a man wife and learned; nor a fuperficial manner of reading them over, or even making extracts from them, by way of a common *memorandum* book, that will enable us to fpeak pertinently upon fubjects, of which we wifh to have the appearance to be mafters. Nothing but a fund in the memory, a large ftock of good obfervations, and the

real

real *bafis* of knowledge, gained by diligence and experience carefully gathered and laid up there, can enable us to fet up as traders in literature. Otherwife, we fuppofe ourfelves to be great fcholars in the fame manner as an empty, vain-glorious man, whom *Seneca* mentions, did: *(Calvifius Sabinus)*. As he was rich, he hired into his houfe feveral fervants, that were well qualified in feveral forts of *learning;* and on *this ftock* he fet up for a perfon of *erudition;* fo that he could refolve by them almoft any queftion in the circle of literature that was ftarted amongft his vifitants.

Juft fo may be faid, that the relying on books, the product of writing on Paper, gives the mind a turn to an indolent habit; and takes it off from that induftrious purfuit and attention, by which a mature knowledge of arts and fciences are the moft properly and furely gained. This objection muft be allowed in its full force, but

never-

neverthelefs the knowledge of letters cannot be the real caufe of fuch indolence, or
deficiency in the improvement of our natural powers and faculties. The noble
inventions of Paper and writing can, therefore, by no means be accufed of encouraging floth or negligence; but, if it be
made a right ufe of, it is undeniably of
fpecial affiftance to mankind in their
literary purfuits and acquifitions. For
where is the memory, however well cultivated, that does not fail the owner fometimes in particular circumftances? and
then to have recourfe to the fubfidiary
aid of writing on Paper, muft be allowed
to be of fingular advantage. A perfon may
fometimes remember very well a quotation,
or a ftory, but may, even for the moment,
not be able to recollect the author's name,
which is often required to an illuftration;
is in fuch inftance a good library therefore
not a beneficial refource? Is here not fully
proved the ufefulnefs of Paper and Writing?

ting? Let none, therefore, lay that blame upon the ufe thereof, which more juftly belongs to their own wrong way of rea-foning; for it can no way encourage idle-nefs, but rather opens and exhibits an ample field, in which the induftrious may advantageoufly employ themfelves with ho-nour and credit, if it be applied to the various good purpofes for which it is moft truly adapted.

Mr. *Robert More* gives a definition of writing in the following words: *Writing,* (fays he, in his fhort effay upon the inven-tion thereof,) *is fuch a reprefentation of our words, but more permanent, as our words are (or ought to be) of our thoughts.* He ftates that the various combinations of twenty-four letters (and none of them repeated) will amount to

620,448,401,733,239,439,360,000.*

* Thefe figures are right; and I join here, for the ufe of thofe who wifh to be informed, the calculation,

which

Writing, in the moft ancient language

that

---

which is done by multiplying all the twenty-four
figures one with another.

$$
\begin{array}{r}
1 \\
\text{by} \ 2 \\
\hline
2 \\
\text{by} \ 3 \\
\hline
6 \\
\text{by} \ 4 \\
\hline
24 \\
\text{by} \ 5 \\
\hline
120 \\
\text{by} \ 6 \\
\hline
720 \\
\text{by} \ 7 \\
\hline
5040 \\
\text{by} \ 8 \\
\hline
40320 \\
\text{by} \ 9 \\
\hline
362880 \\
\text{by} \ 10 \\
\hline
3628800 \\
\text{by} \ 11 \\
\hline
39916800 \\
\text{by} \ 12 \\
\hline
479001600 \\
\text{by} \ 13 \\
\hline
6227020800 \\
\text{by} \ 14 \\
\hline
87178291200
\end{array}
$$

that we know of, is called *Dikduk* דקדוק,
which

$$
\begin{array}{r}
87178291200 \\
\text{by} \qquad 15 \\
\hline
1307674368000 \\
\text{by} \qquad 16 \\
\hline
20922789888000 \\
\text{by} \qquad 17 \\
\hline
355687428096000 \\
\text{by} \qquad 18 \\
\hline
6402373705728000 \\
\text{by} \qquad 19 \\
\hline
121645100408832000 \\
\text{by} \qquad 20 \\
\hline
2432902008176640000 \\
\text{by} \qquad 21 \\
\hline
51090942171709440000 \\
\text{by} \qquad 22 \\
\hline
1124000727777607680000 \\
\text{by} \qquad 23 \\
\hline
25852016738884976640000 \\
\text{by} \qquad 24 \\
\hline
620,448,401,733,239,439,360,000
\end{array}
$$

Clavius, the Jesuit, who also computed these combinations, makes the number to be but

5,852,616,738,497,664,000

which seems to be an error of the press, and that he calculates only 23 letters in his alphabet, and the misprinting appears only in a few figures

25,852,016,738,884,976,640,000

which it is faid fignifies *a fubtle invention;*
and fo it really is, and appears to be, if
we do but reflect, as *Tully* obferves in
his *Tufculan Queftions,* that the *founds of*
the voice, which are in a manner infinite,
are reprefented by a few marks or characters,
which we call letters. Thefe letters in Hebrew are called *Othioth,* אותיות, that is,
Signs; being the figns, or reprefentations
of our words, as is expreffed in the fore-
going definition.

But it may not be amifs here to take
notice, that it is not abfolutely neceffary
that there fhould be juft fuch a precife
number of letters, twenty-four, neither
more or lefs, to exprefs all the words in
a language. The alphabets of various
languages fhew the contrary. The *Hebrew,*
Samaritan, and *Syriac,* have twenty-two;
the *Arabic,* twenty-eight; the *Perfic,* and
Egyptian or *Coptic,* thirty-two; the prefent *Ruffian,* forty-one; the *Malabar,* fifty-
one;

one; the *Japanese* have three alphabets, and forty-eight letters; the *Chinese* have no alphabet, but use near eighty thousand characters; the Greeks are supposed to have had but sixteen letters at the first. But the ingenious *Wachter,* in his *Naturæ & Scripturæ Concordia,* has formed a scheme to shew, that ten characters, the number of our fingers, are sufficient for the expressing of all words in all languages; as ten figures, 1, 2, 3, 4, 5, 6, 7, 8, 9, 0, are sufficient to all calculations. As this invention of Mr. *Wachter* is at least a curiosity, I have here inserted it.

Con-

CONSPECTUS ALPHABETI NATURALIS

Ex Wachteri Naturæ & Scripturæ Concordia, page 64.

GENUS.	FIGURA.	POTESTAS.
Vocal	◯	a, e, i, o, u.
Guttur	♀	k, c, ch, q, g, h.
Lingual	∠	l.
Lingual	⊿	d, t.
Lingual	⊃	r.
Dental	⊓	s.
Labial	3	b, p.
Labial	η	m.
Labial	℞	f, ph, v, w.
Nafal	∧	n.

The art of writing was for a long time entirely unknown in Germany, until the reign

reign of the Emperor *Charles the Great,*
and made even very little progreſs for a
number of years after his reign. Contracts
and deeds were only regiſtered in very
extraordinary caſes, and in general confided
to the memory of authentic and reſpectable
perſons; and in the preſent time, there is
in no country written more than in Germany, which is proved by about one hundred thouſand new publications annually;
which conſume a vaſt quantity of Paper.

Having ſhortly noticed the letters invented and adopted for writing and printing, and conveying ideas, ſentiments, and
improvements in arts and ſciences from one
to another, I will now give a brief account
of the inſtruments and materials which
have been made uſe of, before I proceed
to a hiſtory of the materials which have
been engraved, printed, and written on.

The

The inftruments were of two kinds; they performed their fervices either immediately or by the affiftance of fluids. To the firft belong the wedge, (*cuneus*); the chiffel, (*celtes, celten, coellum, caelum*); and the writing fefcue, (*ftilus, graphium*). And to the fecond, the writing reed, (*calamus fcriptorius*, or *calamus chartarius*); the pencil; and the quills or pens.

The wedge and the chiffel are the moft ancient writing inftruments; the firft inhabitants of the globe formed therewith in wood, ftone, and on metal and wax, their images, or reprefentations, hieroglyphicks, and at laft their alphabetical letters, which have been mentioned in the Bible in feveral places; (Job, ch. xix. v. 23, 24. Jeremiah, ch. xvii. v. 1.) On thofe followed the writing-fefcue, which was ufually made from iron, and fometimes from ivory, copper, filver, &c. Genteel perfons ufed in general, fefcues

of

of filver, of which one has been found of
Childerich. Thofe of ivory or bone were
ufed to write on wood and wax; and
thofe made of iron for writing on leaden
and copper plates.

Thefe fefcues were of different fhapes;
fometimes large and ftrong; and fmall and
thin, for other purpofes; fome were of the
fhape of pins or needles; but one end
was ufually blunt and broad, to efface the
mifwritten letters and words, which were
named by the Romans, *ftilum vertere.*
Some fefcues were fo large, that they
could be ufed for the fame purpofes as
ftilettos; and feveral authors have noticed,
that in many inftances they have been
employed for committing murder. But it
is doubtful, if this be the reafon, why
the ufe thereof has been entirely prohibited for fome time in Rome. It would
be a ftrange interdiction; and as fingular
as a prohibition of cords and knives, becaufe

caufe they have been fometimes employed for committing murder and fuicide.

But fuch fefcues were too fharp for writing on parchment and Egyptian paper, for which reafon reeds were employed for thofe purpofes. Pliny fays, that the ancients gave the preference to Egyptian reed, (*cognatione quadam papyri*.) Yet many other reeds have been ufed; and Martinus Crufius ftates, that the writing reeds from Perfia were generally ufed. When fuch reeds became blunt by ufe, they were either fharpened with a knife, or on a rough ftone, and fuch re-pointed reed was named by Cicero *calamum temperatum*.

The reeds were fplit on the points, like our pens, to lay the colour or ink neater on the paper or parchment, for which reafon Aufonius names them *diffipedes*. According to Chardin, the ufe of reeds is ftill continued in feveral Oriental countries,

tries, and not fuperceded by the introduction of quills. Goguet and others maintain that pencils have been ufed for writing
prior to the introduction of reeds, but
nothing can be pofitively afcertained, except that reeds have been always more
abundantly in ufe than pencils. The
Chinefe continue ftill to ufe hair-pencils
for painting their letters. Their ink-ftand
is a polifhed piece of marble, with a hole
in one corner containing water, in which
they dip a piece of ink, and rub it on
the marble more or lefs, according as they
wifh to make the ftrokes more black or
brighter. They hold the pencil perpendi-
cular, and write from the right to the left,
from the top to the bottom. The marble,
paper, pencil, and ink, which are all their
writing inftruments and materials, are
jointly named *pau-tfe*.

Rauwolff tells us in his Travels, p. 87,
(Augfburg, 1573,) that in the Turkifh
dominions,

dominions, in the fhops, canes (for pens)
are to be fold, which are fmall and hol-
low within, fmooth without, and of a
brownifh red colour, wherewith the Turks
and Moors write : for to write with goofe-
quills is not in ufe with them. Tavernier alfo, in one of his voyages, p. 229,
tells us, that the Perfians ufe three forts of
hands: fet-hand, court-hand, and running-
hand; and that they write with fmall Indian reeds, bearing their hands exceeding
lightly. Their ink, he fays, is made of
galls and charcoal, pounded together with
foot; but their paper is coarfe and brown,
being made of cotton fuftian. Sir John
Chardin, in his Travels, vol. ii. p. 108, &c.
likewife obferves, that the Perfians, who
write from the right hand to the left, hold
their paper in their hands, and do not
lean upon tables or defks, as we do, and
perform their work with dexterity. Worm,
in his Mufeum, p. 164 and 383, tells us,
that the inhabitants of Malacca write from

the

the left hand to the right, as we do, upon
the leaves of palm trees, some of which
are two cubits long, two inches broad,
and as thick as parchment; they make
their letters, by pricking the leaf with an
iron ſtyle, which they hold in their right
hand, while the leaf is held in the left.
The Turks in like manner, who employ a
great number of clerks, as they permit
no printing amongſt them, according to
the aforeſaid Rauwolff's teſtimony, oftener
write upon their knees than upon deſks
or tables.

The introduction of quills, of which we
make at preſent our writing pens, according to Iſidorus, Montfaucon, and Schwarz,
is only one thouſand two or three hundred
years ſince ; and thoſe who ſay that it has
been noticed by Juvenal are as erroneous
as Chriſt, who, in his treatiſe on Literature and Antiquities, ſtates, p. 321,
that pens made of quills are only two or

D   three

three hundred years in ufe. In the imperial library at Vienna is a picture, exhibited as a great curiofity, of Ariftotle's writing with a quill; and in Rome is the ftatue from which this picture is copied, with a manufcript, written in 1471. If that had been written in Ariftotle's time, the ftatue would have been moft likely carved with a reed inftead of a quill. Ifidorus Hifpalenfis, who lived about the middle of the feventh century, is the firft who ufed the word *penna* for a writing pen.

Let me here obferve, that wherever the word pen occurs in our Englifh tranflation of the Old and New Teftament, we muft not underftand it of a pen made of a quill, but of an iron ftyle, or a reed; for though our name pen be derived from the Latin *penna*, yet this latter is never ufed for a pen to write with, in the Roman claffics. Bayle, in his dictionary,

tionary, relates a remarkable particular of
Leo Allatius, that he having made ufe of
one and the fame pen for forty years, in
writing Greek, and lofing it at laft, was
ready to cry for grief; but he does not
inform us what that pen was made of,
nor whether he did not make ufe of
fome others between whiles. To give an
inftance nearer home of a fimilar cafe,
Philemon Holland, a phyfician of Coventry,
tranflated Pliny's Natural Hiftory into Englifh with one pen, as he fays himfelf in
thefe lines:

> With one fole pen, I wrote this book,
>   Made of a grey-goofe quill;
> A pen it was when I it took,
>   A pen I leave it ftill.

The author of the Hiftory of Manual Arts,
8vo. p. 61, fays, that a lady, whofe name
he mentions not, preferved this identical
pen in a filver cafe; fo that it poffibly
may remain in fome mufeum of curiofi-
ties to this day.

In

In all ſtationery ſhops in this country are now exhibited for ſale various pens made of gold and ſilver, ſome of which are very uſeful, containing ink in ſuch a manner, that a perſon, by ſhaking it, is at all times able to write on promenades and travelling, or in libraries, picture galleries, naturaliſts cabinets, &c. which is much preferable to the writing with black-lead pencils, which rubs out and is obliterated. The mechanic Scheller in Leipſic makes a ſuperior kind. Neverthelefs, pens made of gooſe-quills remain in common uſe, the conſumption of which is now very great in all countries, and are imported in many countries to a conſiderable amount. Is it, therefore, not ſurprizing that no greater attention is paid to breed geeſe more abundantly, as they provide not only pens to write with, but alſo feathers for our beds to repoſe easily, and wholeſome food for our ſupport?

In

In the library of the Duke of Brunſ-
wick at Wolfenbuttle is an old Greek
manuſcript of the four Evangeliſts, in
which the pictures of St. Matthew and
St. Mark are painted with beautiful colours on a gilt ground. All the ancient
writing utenſils are here more diſtinct
than in any other work. The ink-ſtand
is therein of a black colour, and cloſe to
it a veſſel which ſeems to contain a red
liquid.

The ſand-box or glaſs was likewiſe a
writing utenſil of the ancients. But they
joined alſo another veſſel or glaſs, filled
with a liquid, to attenuate the ink.

The feſcue and reed had always a ſeparate conſervatory, to prevent their being
damaged, which was named by the Latins
theca calamaria, and *graphiarium*. A
puncher was uſually joined, which ſerved
to point out the commencement and

end

end of each line, and fometimes the large letters.

The rule, *regula, norma, canon,* was ufually a feparate utenfil, but fometimes joined in the confervatory. It was ufed to draw lines, and to divide the fheets of parchment into *columns.* The lines were drawn with an inftrument, fimilar to a demi-circle, with a handle, and leaden or iron points. The fame inftrument, if of iron, ferved likewife for cutting the parchment or paper. If it was too fharp, it often cut the parchment. This inftrument was named *fubula.* Blank lines, drawn either with the fefcue or with the *fubula,* are difcovered in all neatly written ancient manufcripts, and in many records from the fixth to the fourteenth century. The pierced points difcovered on both ends of the lines were made with the before mentioned puncher.

Pumice

Pumice (*pumex*) was likewife a writing material of the ancients, and ufed to fmooth the rough and uneven parts of the parchment, or to fharpen the reed. Pumice has been likewife ufed in modern times to erafe entirely ancient writings, to the deftruction of valuable manufcripts, which parchments were again fmoothened, and often fcribbled over with inconfequent ftuff, or of lefs note than it contained formerly, which is the origin of *codices refcripti*. But if the ink had funk too much in the parchment, remnants of the old letters remained, as is to be feen in the library at Wolfenbuttle, where is preferved an old piece of parchment, from which the Epiftle to the Romans was erafed, and the copyift had written the Origines of the Bifhop Ifidorus.

A fponge ferved to rub out fuch letters as were written by miftake or inattention on the parchment, and to wipe off or to

cleanfe

cleanfe the writing reed. Parchment or
paper was cut either with paper-fciffars,
or the before mentioned *fubula*; and all
lines were feparated at an equal diftance
with a compafs.

The ink that the ancients wrote with,
was of various kinds, in the compofition
and colours, as we have it now. Black, as
at prefent, was the moft common; for that
reafon the Latins called it, *melan*, *atra-
mentum*. Diofcorides, Pliny, Vitruvius,
and Ifodorus have acquainted us with the
different preparations of the ink which
the ancients ufed, which are not at all
fimilar to the prefent. Pliny fays, that
the Romans made their ink of foot, taken
from furnaces and baths. Some alfo wrote
with the black liquid that is found in the
fepia, or cuttle-fifh. Dalechamp, in a
note upon the aforefaid chapter of Pliny,
obferves, that the northern nations, (without explaining which he means by that
term)

term) write very well with the said liquid, by adding a little alum to it. Jacob
Quandt describes the ink of the ancient
Hebrews, and in the Canaparius* published
at Venice in 1619, are published a great
number of receipts for making the ink
of the ancients.

Persius, the poet, in the following verses,
translated by Mr. Dryden, humorously
describes a lazy young student, laying the
blame of his own idleness upon his writing materials; where he metaphorically
puts *sepia* for ink, and uses three different
words, in the compass of four lines, viz.
calamus, arundo, and fistula, for a pen.

> With much ado, his book before him laid,
> And parchment with the smoother side display'd;
> He takes the papers, lays 'em down again,
> And with unwilling fingers tries his pen;
>
> Some

---

* This book is written in bad Latin, and describes
numerous chemical experiments, and was therefore
re-published at London in 1660; and at Rotterdam in
1718.

Some peevifh quarrel ftraight he ftrives to pick,
His quill writes double, or his ink's too thick;
Infufe more water; now 'tis grown too thin,
It finks, nor can the charaɛters be feen.

The firft ink was made of red wine,
concentrated by boiling, and of mufk
named *fapa*; fince of mulberry juice;
but principally of foot, tempered with
fome glue or gum, and fometimes, for
the prefervation of paper and parchment,
with an extraɛt from wormwood. The
Chinefe make ink from lamp-black, obtained by burning different materials, principally of fir wood and oil, of which they
make a pafte and dry it. All ink made of
foot, changed in the courfe of time, its
black colour into yellow, as appears by
many ancient manufcripts. But we muft
not form a decided opinion on the colour
of ink with which manufcripts have been
written; becaufe we find, in almoft all
manufcripts of the firft fourteen centuries,
letters of different colours, from the paleft

to

to the darkeſt ; and Wanſley juſtly obſerves, that amongſt ancient manuſcripts, of one thouſand years and upwards old, are found ſome written with ink yet darker black than any which we now are able to make. We cannot, therefore, rejeɑt the antiquity of a diploma, becauſe it reſembles our modern ink.

Our anceſtors uſed not only black ink, but alſo red ink of different ſhades and qualities, which was made of ruddle, *rubrica;* red lead, *minium;* the juice of kermes, *coccus;* or of vermilion, *cinnabaris;* and ſometimes purple ink, which was made, with a particular treatment, from boiled purple ſnails, and their pulverized ſhells.

Purple ink was very expenſive, and therefore not much uſed*. The writing
therewith

---

* The knowledge of the ingredients uſed by the ancients in making purple was loſt with the conqueſt
of

therewith became in later times a pre-
rogative of the Emperors, that colour
being a token of dignity, grandeur, and
fublimity. The oriental Emperors figned
their edicts and mandates with purple ink,
for which reafon it was named *facrum
encauftum;* and as late as the twelfth century, they divided that honour with their
next relations. The Emperor Leo inter-
dicted the ufe of the *facrum encauftum* to
all private perfons and noblemen; and
the regents who governed the ftate, during
the minority of an Emperor, ufed not
purple, but green ink for their fignature.
Montfaucon notices fome Imperial figna-
tures with *facro encaufto,* which is greatly
different

---

of Conftantinople, becaufe the purple-manufactures
were, fince the reign of Theodofius, the great private property of the Emperors, and therefore there
remained only one at Tyre, and another at Conftantinople. The former place was deftroyed by the
Saracens and the other by the Turks; and thus this
art, with which only a few perfons were acquainted,
has been loft, and not yet again difcovered.

different from the *encauſtum* uſed by the
Greeks and Romans for painting.

Joſephus ſays, the Jews had their *thora*
with golden letters; and Hieronymus mentions that in his time has been written
with gold; which yet is copiouſly done
in Egypt, according to Maillet's deſcription of Egypt, vol. 2. p. 192. It is well
known, that the Perſians, when they write
to their ſuperiors, to whom they wiſh
to ſhew in their letters high veneration,
write on white paper with gold flowers;
and they paint the name and title with
gold letters.

The gold ink has been prepared different ways; the cuſtomary method has
been, to mix pure gold and ſilver in a
crucible over the fire, adding porphyrian
marble and ſulphur, after it has been
converted into fine powder, and digeſted
over a ſlow fire in an earthen well-covered
veſſel.

veffel. The whole was then put into the fame well-covered earthen veffel, and kept on a flow fire until it was red. When cold, it was pounded in a marble mortar, with plenty of water; when fettled, that water was poured off, and other water ufed until it was found thoroughly clean. If wanted for ufe, a part thereof was taken the day before, and fome gum and water added, and, when ufed, made milk-warm.

Conftantine the Great ordered fair-hand-writers to make fifty copies of the Bible on parchment, under the direction of the Bifhops Cæfarea and Eufebius, which have been fince copied at different times with gold letters by command of his fuc-ceffors.

At Hervorden is preferved a manu-fcript written with gold letters, found in the grave of Wittekind.

In

In the cathedral of Aix la Chapelle is
a part of the New Teſtament written
with golden letters. It was put into the
grave of Charles the Great at the time
of his burial, but the Emperor Otto the
Third ordered it to be taken out in the
year 1000, which was 186 years after
the death of Charles. This book is remarkable, becauſe, the Emperors of the
Roman empire are bound at their coronation to make their oath by laying
their fingers on the firſt page of St.
John the evangeliſt. It is in a large
quarto ſize, and was elegantly bound 400
years after the death of Charles the Great,
and is, with the cover, about three inches
thick. The leaves are all of a violet-
colour, and the gold colour of the letters
is tolerably well preſerved. The book
contains the writings of the four evangeliſts; but all that which belongs not
to the text, is written with ſilver letters,
and not ſo well preſerved. The whole

is

is very neat, but not divided into chapters and verſes; it is *in una ſerie*, without any ſtops, points, or other marks of diſtinction; without capital letters or ornaments: the letters are however all of one ſize, and the words without abbreviations. It ſeems to be written either at the latter end of the eighth, or the commencement of the ninth century. The ſeveral accounts given of this book are contradictory. Koehler erroneouſly aſſerts that it is written on bark-paper, but it is certain, and I am eye-witneſs by examination, that the leaves are thin parchment. If this book has not been taken away before Aix la Chapelle was Frenchified, I am at a loſs to know in what manner any future Emperor can be conſtitutionally crowned, becauſe, according to the conſtitution of Germany, ſeveral inſignia are required at the coronation of an Emperor, which are gathered together from ſeveral places, and brought ſolemnly

to

to Francfort on the Main for the ufe of the coronation.

Another book of the Evangelifts with golden letters is in the convent of St. Emeran, at Regenfburgh : it is on one fide with gilt plate, ornamented with diamonds; and given by the Emperor Arnolphus to the holy Emeran, before he died. It is publicly exhibited in the church of the convent on all holy days.

In the Imperial library at Vienna, and in the library of the convent of St. Gallen, are the Pfalms of David, written with golden letters. In the laft century, there was, in the library of the Monkhoufe family, near Schaumbourg, the whole Bible written in golden letters, given to that family by Sophia the Firft, Abbefs of Ganderfheim, daughter of Otto the Second. And in the year 1788, Ettingen, a book-feller of reputation at Gotha, offered for fale

E   a very

a very neat manufcript, containing fome chapters of the Alcoran, written with gold letters, in the Arabic language.

The following records are further pre-ferved. The diploma of Otto the Second, in the archive of the minifter at Gander-fheim. A record of the Emperor Henry the Second, in the bifhopric of Paderborn in Weftphalia. Another of Conrad the Third; and one of the Emperor Frederick the Firft; both in the abbey of Corvey. And in the three confirmation bulls, of the privileges of the church of Rome, given by the Emperors Otto the Firft and the Second, and Henry the Saint; and further, in the marriage compact of the Emperor Otto the Second with Theophania; and in the chart of Lotharius the Second, which he delivered to the Abbot Wiblo at Stavelot, the gold has not been fpared.

In the vaults of a deftroyed temple at Semipalat,

Semipalat*, in Siberia, have been found
feveral rolls of blue and black coloured
paper, entirely written on, with gold letters. They were delivered to the Czar
Peter the Great, who could not difcover
in his empire one fingle perfon who was
able either to read or to tranflate thefe
neatly written and well-preferved manufcripts. One of thefe rolls was therefore
fent to Paris by Schumacher, librarian of
the academy at Mofcow, to the Abbot
Bignon, who was in great repute, and
was librarian to the King of France, foli-
citing him to find out a learned perfon,
who was able to ftate in what language
the roll had been written, and to develope
the contents. The Abbot Bignon fhewed
it to Fourmont, interpreter to the king,
who was faid to be mafter of the Chinefe
and

* Semipalat, which is fituated on the river Upper
Irtifch, ftill retains its name, and that from feven palates,
or apartments, which are there among the ruins.

and other oriental languages. This bold
grammarian, who had never before feen
fimilar letters, and relying in full confi-
dence on the fame of his great knowledge
of the oriental languages, led by vanity,
had the impudence to hold out, that he
was the only perfon capable of tranflating
the writing. He afferted, it was written
in the ancient Tangutian language, and
delivered a fictitious tranflation, compofed
by his own fancy. Peter the Great, who
doubted the correctnefs of the tranflation,
neverthelefs made him a very confiderable
prefent, and thereby encreafed his fame.
But in the reign of the Emprefs Ann,
many years after the death of Peter the
Great, two Ruffians appeared at the academy of St. Peterfburgh, who, during a
refidence of fixteen years in Pekin, had
learned the Chinefe and Mantfchurian languages. They recognized immediately,
that the writings of all the rolls were in
the Mantchurian language; they read
them

them without hefitation and difficulty; they tranflated feveral, and amongft others the roll, formerly tranflated by the French- man Fourmont. But not a fingle word agreed with his tranflation; and it was fully afcertained, that Fourmont had been an impoftor, who did not know a fingle letter of the roll. The original rolls are ftill preferved in the academy of fciences at St. Peterfburgh, with both tranflations; and are, according to Jacob von Stæhlein, permitted to be feen by every one who enquires for them.

Similar rolls of fmoothed blue paper, written in part with golden, and in part with golden and filver letters, with the holy characters of the Tibetans, were in Sloane's library, and marked with the numbers 2836 and 2837. They were found beyond Siberia, in the fouth-eaftern part of Tartary.

Manu-

Manufcripts written with filver letters
are more fcarce. A few are yet exifting
One of Gregorius Nazianzenus was in the
King's library at Paris, wherein all quo-
tations from the holy Scriptures were
written with golden letters, and all other
parts in filver. The Pfalter of David
is in the library at Zurich, written with
filver letters on purple-coloured parchment in the feventh century: the title
is written with golden letters. The manufcript of the Gothic tranflation of the
four books of the evangelifts, by the Bifhop
Ulphilas, who lived in the year 350, is
preferved at the univerfity of Upfal. All
the letters are filver, except the capitals,
which are gold. According to Mabillon
and Gatterer, diplomas written with filver
letters are not in exiftence.

It is of confequence to mankind in
general that writings may be preferved;
which depends on the ftrength of paper
and

and parchment, and on fuch a durable black ink, as will not fade by age, nor obliterate in water. Aftle, in his Origin and Progrefs of Writing, fays, " It is an " objeƈt of the utmoft importance that " the records of parliament, the decifions " and adjudications of the courts of juf- " tice, conveyances from man to man, " wills, teftaments, and other inftruments, " which affeƈt property, fhould be written " with ink of fuch durable quality, as " may beft refift the deftruƈtive power " of time and elements. The neceffity " of paying greater attention to this matter " may be readily feen, by comparing the " rolls and records, which have been writ- " ten from the fifteenth century to the " end of the feventeenth, with the writings " we have remaining of various ages from " the fifth to the twelfth centuries. Not- " withftanding the fuperior antiquity of " the latter, they are in excellent pre- " fervation; but we frequently find the

" former.

" former, though of modern date, fo
" much defaced, that they are fcarcely
" legible."

Several experienced chymifts have endeavoured to difcover a durable black ink,
and to prepare paper for lafting writings;
which induces me to acquaint the publick with their proceffes. Lambert recommends " to pound the gall-nuts in an
" iron mortar to very fine powder, and
" to pour three or four times its quan-
" tity of water on it; to let it remain
" eight or ten days in the fun, or to
" boil it for half an hour or longer, ac-
" cording to the quantity. To diffolve
" iron-vitriol, to be ftrained and added
" to the diffolution of galls, till the ink
" attains the defired black colour. Too
" fmall a quantity of vitriol produces a
" brown reddifh colour; if more be added,
" a violet; then a black hue, and at laft
" a dark black. If the colour of the
" ink

" ink be not fufficiently dark, he re-
" commends to thicken it by boiling, and
" then to add gum in fuch a quantity
" that the ink may be neither too fluid
" nor too tough." The ink is always of a
fuperior quality, if made fufficiently aqueous
when prepared, becaufe by adding water
a portion of the fine black particles will
precipitate. Lambert defines not the
quantity of the ingredients, and they are
not always of the fame quality. Lewis
propofes to take three ounces of galls
to one ounce of iron-vitriol; but Lambert
recommends to take lefs vitriol, to prevent
the paper from turning yellow. Experience proves daily, that with one and the
fame ink written on different paper, different fhades of black are produced ; and
this muft originate in the lime and glue
ufed in the paper-mill, or if the paper
or rag has been bleached by a chymical
procefs. An ink which as far as it poffibly can be done retains its dark colour

on

on every kind of paper, is the moſt preferable.

Auguſtus Lewis Pfannenſmith in Hanover has invented a black ink, which,
by trial, is found to be ſuperior to all
others: it is different from all other inks
hitherto known, becauſe,

1. It is entirely made from ſuch pro-
ductions of the country, as can be procured abundantly and cheap, without
uſing galls and gum.

2. The writing done with this ink
cannot be deſtroyed, by oil of vitriol,
ſpirit of ſalt, ſpirit of nitre, ſalt of lemon,
ſalt of forrel; nor by any alkalies, which
can only alter its colour in a ſmall degree, either yellowiſh or reddiſh.

3. The writings with this ink alter not
by time, or if expoſed to the air and heat
of the ſun.

4. It.

4. It can be prepared like the Chinefe ink in dry cakes, and is therefore convenient for exportation and travellers.

It's preparation is as follows: " One
" peck of foot, and one and a half peck
" of wood-afhes, is to be boiled with four
" or five pails of foft water, whereby the
" alkaline falts extracted from the afhes
" diffolve all thofe parts of the foot
" which are capable of diffolution. This
" is poured altogether into an empty
" hogfhead, and filled up with water; it
" muft remain there for twenty-four
" hours, conftantly ftirring the clear li-
" quid, which is of a brown colour; it is
" then drawn into another cafk of the
" fame fize. About thirty or forty pounds
" of oak bark, with four or five pounds
" of Brazil wood fhavings*, are to be
" boiled during three or four hours with
" as much water as is fufficient to cover
                                    " the

* This wood is not abfolutely neceffary.

" the ingredients. The extract is to be
" filtered through a cloth, and put into
" another veſſel. Six pounds of iron of
" vitriol is to be diſſolved in ſix pounds of
" ſoft water. To this diſſolution is to be
" added a pail full of cold water, and put
" into the caſk which contains the brown
" liquid. The alkaline ſalts extracted
" from the aſhes which were neceſſary
" to diſſolve the foot, and from the ex-
" tracted vitriolic acids, mix with the
" water ; and the diſſolved parts of the
" foot, the iron and earthy parts of the
" vitriol, with the colour and gum ex-
" tracted from the oak bark and Brazil
" wood ſhavings, form a mixed precipitate.
" It is therefore required to ſeparate the
" alkaline lie from the acid, which is
" accompliſhed by adding as much clean
" water as is required to fill the hogſhead.
" It muſt be well ſtirred, and left three
" or four days to ſettle, in which time
" the united precipitate is ſettled at the
" bottom.

" bottom. The clean water on the top
" muft then be drawn off, and thrown
" away. The cafk is then to be filled
" again with frefh water, fo far as to
" receive one pail full of water more. In
" the pail with water required to fill the
" cafk, twelve ounces of iron-vitriol is to
" be diffolved, which is ftirred and
" poured into the hogfhead. The laft
" procefs is neceffary to facilitate the
" fecond precipitation, which is otherwife
" more difficult than at the firft time.
" Within two days it is again fettled;
" the water is then to be drawn off from
" the top. A wooden frame muft be pre-
" pared, on which is flackly to be faftened
" a piece of half-bleached fine linen cloth;
" the frame muft then be placed on fup-
" porters as horizontally as poffibly can
" be done, and a pail full of the preci-
" pitated colour is then flowly to be poured
" upon the ftraining cloth. Some coloured
" liquid will at firft run through, which
" muft

" muſt be ſaved, but the clear water which
" comes afterwards is to be ſuffered to run
" away ; then continue to add more of the
" precipitate, as much as the ſtrainer will
" hold, and only clear water will drain off.
" Within two or three days the colour
" appears on the cloth, reſembling pap,
" which is to be taken off, and well ſtirred
" with a few pails full of clean water in
" a wooden tub, and again poured into
" the hogſhead, which is again to be filled
" with clean water, and twelve ounces of
" iron-vitriol added in the ſame manner
" as heretofore deſcribed. The whole is
" then ſtirred, time is given to precipitate,
" and the colour ſtrained on the frame.
" The reaſon, why (throughout the whole
" of this proceſs) it is preſcribed to uſe re-
" peatedly ſuch a large quantity of water,
" is to clean the diſſolved foot as much as
" poſſible, and to obtain the united preci-
" pitate from the extract of the oak-bark
" and the iron-vitriol in the fineſt ſtate,
" which

" which principally contributes to the
" durability of this ink, and impreffes
" deeper into the interftices of the
" paper. The repeated adding and draw-
" ing off of the water is neceffary to
" carry off the vitriolic acid as much as
" poffibly can be done. Now, for the
" laft time, take the ink-pap from the
" frame and add an alkaline-lie, prepared of
" two pounds or two pounds and an half of
" American pot afh, diffolved in the fame
" weight of water, and fix ounces of com-
" mon falt diffolved in water, which is to
" be heated altogether in a boiler, con-
" ftantly ftirring it. If to this is added
" fix quarts of malt-vinegar, well ftirred,
" a very durable and good ink is obtained.
" The flimy parts of the vinegar are of
" ufe in this preparation. Should it happen
" that the ink prepared in this manner
" should turn out of a yellowifh shade,
" the foot has been of too rich a colour,
" and there should have been taken lefs

" in

" in proportion to the colour extracted
" from the oak-bark. The laft directed
" ufe of pot afh, which in the firft part
" of the procefs has been prefcribed to
" detach, ferves now to diffolve again all
" the parts of the foot yet remaining in
" the mixed precipitate, and thereby to
" give the ink a greater power to imprefs
" into the paper; and to promote the
" durability of the colour, ferving at the
" fame time as gum. To form this ink
" into cakes, a number of flat ftones
" fhould be placed in fuch a manner,
" that they may be eafily heated. Some
" of the ink is to be poured thereupon;
" and when evaporated more is to be
" added, conftantly ftirring until formed
" like a pafte, which is to be taken from
" the ftone plates, and laid on a warm
" place, till fufficiently dried. If wanted
" for ufe the cakes are to be pulverized,
" and converted into good ink, by the addi-
" tion of fome boiling water."

To

To prepare paper for lafting writings is a valuable addition in the art of making paper; and the new manufactory, now building at Millbank, for manufacturing paper from ftraw and other vegetables, will be fhortly in a ftate to provide the publick fufficiently with paper exprefsly manufactured for that purpofe.

As perhaps the patience of the reader may be tired with the long but neceffary procefs of making an everlafting black ink, I join for his recreation receipts for making the beft and moft lafting coloured inks.

For Red Ink:—Take four ounces pernambuco wood fhavings of the beft quality, boil it with half an ounce of alum in a quart of rain water, during one hour; when ftrained, add a little gum Arabic.

In the fame manner different coloured inks can be made from all known dyeing woods.

F

woods. Yellow-wood will produce yellow ink; Brazil-wood, violet ink, &c. But all inks made from dyeing wood will be more beautiful and lafting, if a fmall diffolution of tin is added to it, which is to be prepared as follows: diffolve in four ounces of the ftrongeft oil of vitriol, half an ounce of fal armoniac, and as much tin as will diffolve; or mix *fpiritus falis* with *fpiritus nitri*, and diffolve in it as much tin fhavings as will diffolve, if it even fhould take up two or three days, which folution, if kept in a glafs phial, will laft many years. All inks made from boiled dyeing wood may be mixed, and thereby obtain numerous fhades of different beautiful colours: but care muft be taken never to ufe in thefe inks a pen dipped in black ink, becaufe the particles of iron, which are a property of black ink, will fpoil all other coloured inks.

For

For Green Ink:—Pound three ounces of verdigreafe and two ounces of white tartar in fixteen ounces of water for twelve or fifteen minutes; when ftrained add two ounces of gum Arabic.

For Blue Ink of the greateft beauty and durability:—Pound two ounces of the beft Pruffian blue (Berlin blue), and pour on it two ounces of fpirit of falt, mixed with two ounces of water: keep it milk-warm, and ftir it till the blue is diffolved, which will take place in three or four hours. The veffel muft not be too fmall, becaufe the mixture will at firft ferment and rife. It is afterwards attenuated with more or lefs water, according to the fhade of blue you wifh to have. No gum Arabic is to be added.

The diplomatics name, befides metals, five other materials, ufed for the impreffion of feals, and for fealing letters and

other

other things, to wit, *terra figillata*, putty,
pafte, wax, and fealing-wax.

Notwithftanding Pliny denies that feals
have been ufed by the ancient Egyptians,
it is neverthelefs proved that they were
well acquainted with the ufe of the
terra figillata, which was, according to
Herodotus, the firft ftuff employed for
that purpofe. He fays, that the Egyptian
priefts bound on the horns of the animals
felected for immolation, a piece of paper,
on which they impreffed their feals on
terra figillata, and thofe animals marked
in that manner could only be taken for
facrifices. Mofes mentions likewife the
feal-ring of Pharaoh. Lucian fays that
all perfons who went to fortune-tellers,
were obliged to write the queries on a
ticket, which muft be folded up and fealed
with wax or *terra figillata*. Cicero, Ser-
vius, and others fay that the fame has
been ufed by the ancients; and it feems
that

that the fame earth has been ufed for fealing by the Byzantine Emperors, becaufe fome perfon attempted to defend the worfhipping of images, by ftating, that no perfon who received a command from the Emperor, and kiffed the feal, did it to fhew veneration to the parchment, the lead, or the *terra figillata,* but to fhew his refpect to the Emperor.

The earth which is now by us named chalk, cannot have been the *creta* of the ancients, which they ufed for fealing, it muft have been of the clay kind, which only takes impreffions, and retains the fame when hardened by drying. That the Latins have often expreffed a kind of clay by the name of *creta* has been proved by Columella, Virgil, Varro and others.

Wax has been ufed for fealing in the moft ancient times in Europe; but whether

white

white or yellow was firft ufed is a
point on which the diplomatics differ.
Gatterer fays that the wax which was firft
ufed for fealing was white, but Beckman declares that the yellow was the firft
and generally ufed, at leaft by private perfons, being the cheapeft; and I cannot
help deciding in his favour, becaufe the
progrefs of arts was very flow in ancient
times, which induces me to believe that
many years paffed before the art of bleach-
ing wax was difcovered. After it was
found out that the yellow colour of wax
could be converted into white, it was
foon coloured red; but green and yellow
wax was not known in Germany before
the fourteenth century.

That the Conftantinopolitan patriarchs,
the high-mafter of the Teutonic-order,
the grand-mafter of the knights of Malta,
and fome of the firft nobility, ufed the
black colour for their feals, is, according
to

to Gatterer, Thulemarius, Heineccius, and
Hanfelman well known; but, that the
mafters of the Templars ufed the fame
colour for fealing, we are informed of
folely by Dr. Chriftopher Smith, otherwife
Phifeldek, who ftates, that there is preferved in the archives of the Duke of
Brunfwic at Wolfenbuttle, a document,
written by Mafter Widekind on parchment, on which hangs a black feal on
blue and white linen thread.

Blue fealing wax was unknown in former
times, notwithftanding it is ftated by
Struvius, that the Emperor Frederick the
Third granted Hans Schenk, Lord at
Tuutenberg; and by Heineccius, that the
Emperor Charles the Fifth granted in 1524
Dr. Stockhammer in Nuremberg, the pri-
vilege to ufe blue wax for their feals.
We may fay, that the art of dyeing wax
blue, is ftill a fecret. No receipt for
making it is to be found in any ancient

F 4   work;

work; and the receipts given by modern authors, by Le Pileur d'Apligny and others, produce no blue, but a dirty colour, which is neither green nor blue. The coloured juices, when united with wax, make it more greeniſh than blue; and if mineral-earths are uſed, they will not unite with wax, and ſettle at the bottom. If therefore a ſeal of blue wax could be produced, of which the external part has not been coloured, ſuch a curi-oſity would puzzle the technologiſts and diplomatics, and be a problem for our chymiſts. The privileges which have been given to Schenk and Stockhammer are therefore ſimilar to other privileges which have been granted in the year 1704 to the county of Reinſtein and the princi-pality of Halberſtadt, not only to work in their mines minerals, but likewiſe indigo. By theſe privileges the Lord and Doctor could find as much blue wax, as the others could melt indigo from ore found

in

in their mines. Neverthelefs, Beckman
does not give up the hope, that the art
of dying wax blue will yet be difcovered,
although all trials have hitherto been unfuccefsful.

The ufe of wafers is more modern
than the ufe of feals; and no ancient
diploma is to be found fealed with wafers.
The moft ancient is not two hundred years
old. Spiefz could not difcover any one
older than of the year 1624 ; but Martin
Schwartner found, in the univerfity library
at Peft, three fomewhat older; one is a
paffport, given by Father Vifitator to three
travelling Jefuits, dated Bruffels 1603;
the impreffion on the wafers is the ufual
infcription on the Jefuit feals.

Pafte has been ufed for fealing letters
before the difcovery of fealing-wax. Some
learned men tell us of a feal-putty, named
maltha, manufactured from combuftible and

rifing

rifing compofitions. If this affertion is founded on truth, it has been the firft and moft ancient fealing-wax. The fealing-wax now in ufe is compofed of fimilar materials, and has fuperfeded all ancient fealing matters by its cheapnefs, convenience, and beautiful appearance, notwithftanding its brittlenefs, and that an impreffion on it can be eafily forged.

The moft ancient mention of fealing-wax in books is found in *Garcia ab orto aromatum & fimplicium aliquot hiftoria,* printed in 1563, where by gum-lac the fticks for fealing letters are noticed. In *Nouveau Traité de Diplom.* t. iv. p. 33, is ftated, that Francis Rouffeau, a Frenchman, was the inventor in 1640. It is faid that Rouffeau, after many years refidence in Perfia and India, returned to France, where he loft all his property by fire, in the latter part of the reign of Lewis the Thirteenth, and then eftablifhed a manufactory for making

making fealing-wax from gum-lac*, which he had learned in India. But this Frenchman is not intitled to the invention, which has been already ufed between the years 1550 and 1560, as can be proved by letters fealed with black and red fealing-wax preferved fince 1554 in the archives at Dillenburgh. Spiefz ftates, that there is one on a diploma of 1563 in Anfpach; and Anton has feen in Goerlitz one of 1561 fealed with red fealing-wax; and another of 1620, with black fealing-wax.

Tavernier

---

* The infect which produces the gum-lac is a red fhield-loufe, *coccus lacca*, not yet defcribed in any natural hiftory known to me. It fticks faft to the branches of the *ticus religiofa, indica, rhamnus jujuba, plafo hort. malab.*, and foon appears on the edge of the body a demi-tranfparent glue-like humidity, which fhortly forms a complete cell. Thefe cells are the gum-lac. The white fubftances which are found in the empty cells are the ftriped hides of the young infects. It is plentiful on both fhores of the river Ganges; and one hundred weight has formerly been fold at Dacca for twelve pounds. The moft preferred is dark red. The inhabitants of thefe countries make rings and beads of gum-lac, which they gild and paint, to ornament the fingers and arms of their wives.

Tavernier mentions the preparation of fealing-wax in the Eaft Indies; and it is probable that the Portuguefe learned the art of making fealing-wax in the oriental countries. Its firft name has been Spanifh wax, and the French ftill call it *cire d'Efpagne*; and it feems that it got the name of fealing-wax fince gum-lac has been ufed in place of common rofin. Without gum-lac no fealing-wax can ftick to well-fized and glazed paper.

Copyifts, illuminators, and book-painters, had full employ before the art of printing was invented; but fo much has been written and printed on this, that it would be ufelefs to notice it in this work; and there are fo many nominations of the ancient writers, that the ftatement of it alone would fill a book. Whoever wifhes to be convinced of this, has only to examine Hermanus Hugo *de prima fcribendi origine*, and the Brunfwic Notices of 1750;

and

and for modern times, full information is to be obtained from Maffey's Origin and Progrefs of Letters. I fhall therefore only notice the names given to the principal writers.

All copyifts were named by the Romans *librarii,* and fometimes *fcribis. Bibliopolae* were perfons who kept a number of fervants to write down their own works and dictations, and copied the works of others. *Calligraphi* were fair hand writers. *Tachygraphi,* quick hand writers, and fometimes fhort hand writers; they were likewife named *exceptores.* Secret writings were defcribed by *kryptographi* or *fteganographi.* The Turks call fecret writings *felam.* Monks replaced afterwards the *librariorum.* Remarks written on the edges of manufcripts were called *gloffemata. Examinantes* were perfons who overlooked the works of the copyifts, to which they figned their names. The art of printing here fhews

its

its great fuperiority, becaufe all copies are the fame as the firft. *Illuminatores* painted fome letters and other ornaments of books.

Of the noble invention of printing*, I likewife pafs, and continue with making fome few obfervations on books and book-binding, and on their being fo much expofed to be deftroyed by moths and worms.

The ancients, according to Pliny, ufed to preferve their parchment, paper, and books from moths, by wafhing them over with cedar or citron oil, which gave them at the fame time an agreeable fcent. Thefe books were named *libri cedrati* or *citrati.* He believes that the prefervation

of

---

* It is furprifing that the art of printing books was not earlier invented, as it is well known that the Romans were in the habit of ftamping the initials of their names on the bread which they fent to the publick ovens for baking, which is certainly a kind of printing.

of the books found in the grave of Numa was folely attributed to this precaution. In modern times, many prefervatives for books againft deftructive infects have been propofed, but none have yet been effective. The Royal Society of Sciences at Gottingen thought it therefore of fufficient confequence to propofe in their affembly at the 10th July, 1773, a premium for July 1774, to be given him who delivered the beft anfwer to the following queftion: How many kind of infects are found which are detrimental to records and books? which of the materials, as pap, glue, leather, wood, thread, paper, &c. were attacked by each kind? and, which is the beft and moft approved remedy, either to preferve records and books againft infects, or to deftroy the infects?

Among the numerous anfwers received, Dr. Herman of Strafburgh obtained the premium, and Flad of Heidelbergh got

the

the *acceſſit.* I will give an abridged extract of their anſwers. Many inſects are
charged with injuring books without doing
miſchief, ſuch are: *acarus, cimex perſonatus,
lepiſma ſaccharina, tinea veſtianella, tinea
pellionella, tinea farcitella, attelabus mollis,
attelabus formicarius,* and *attelabus apiarius;*
of the following it is not yet fully aſcertained if they are guilty or innocent;
1. *termes pulſatorium* named alſo *the ſmall
pumice, the timberſow, the book-louſe,* and
the paper-louſe; 2. *phalangium cancroides;*
3. *blatta orientalis;* 4. *ptinus fur;* 5. *tene-
brio molitor;* and 6. *phalaena, or tenia gra-
nella.* The truly deſtructive inſects are,
*ptinus pertinax, dermeſtes paniceus, dermeſtes
lardarius, dermeſtes pellio,* and *byrrhus mu-
ſaeorum.* To preſerve the records and books
againſt inſects and to deſtroy them, it is
propoſed 1. to aboliſh the binding books
with any wood; 2. to recommend the
bookbinder to uſe glue mixed with alum
in place of paſte; 3. to bruſh all worm-
eaten

eaten wood in the repofitorics of books with oil or lac-varnifh ; 4. to preferve books bound in calf, he recommends to brufh them over with thin lac-varnifh ; 5. no book to lay flat; 6. paper, letters, documents, &c. may be preferved in drawers without any danger, provided the wafers are cut out, and that no pafte, &c. is between them; 7. the bookbinder is not to ufe any woollen cloth, and to wax the thread ; 8. to air and duft the books often; 9. to ufe laths, feparated one from the other one inch, in place of fhelves; 10. to brufh over the infides of book-cafes and the laths with lac-varnifh.

The paper in North America is fpeedily deftroyed by dampnefs and infects, which, on the fuggeftion of an honorary member, Mr. François at Neufchatel, induced the Society of Sciences at Philadelphia, in their Affembly of the 11th May 1785 to offer a premium for the beft anfwer

G   on

on the queſtion: if there was no effectual
remedy to protect paper againſt infects?
This ſociety offered another premium of
twenty-five moidores for the beſt method
of making paper for St. Domingo, which
would reſiſt infects, and requeſted to have
ſamples to prove its quality. Several anſwers and ſamples were received, but all
recommended to mix the ſize, on ſizing,
with ſharp and bitter, or other ingredients
which might kill the infects, to wit,
vinegar, allum, vitriol, ſalt, turpentine,
extract of aloes, tobacco, or wormwood;
camphor, aſafœtida caſtoreum, and arſenic,
either to be uſed in the ſize, or afterwards impregnated by infuſion. But theſe
remedies were all rejected, and conſidered
to be either inſufficient, or pernicious and
dangerous; for which reaſon, the ſociety
renewed their offer, without limiting their
anſwer to a precife time, but without any
ſatisfaction, except that Mr. Arthaud,
Royal Phyſician at Cape François, named

t he

the infects which were the moft deftructive
to paper in thefe countries: *dermeftes fcu-
tellatus, nigro teftaceus, ovatus, glaber, clytris
thorace punctis impreffis, oculis nigris punctatis,
antennis curvatis, apice articulis tribus per-
foliatis compreffis,* which generates in all
feafons during the whole year, and is confidered as the moft dangerous of all paper-
eaters.

To prepare paper for prefervation
againft infects, is likewife an object to
which fome of the proprietors of the new
manufactory now building at Millbank
have paid particular attention; and they
flatter themfelves they will likewife be
able to bring to fale, and to lay before
the examination of fcientific men, and
the publick at large, paper, in this view
much fuperior to any other heretofore
manufactured.

Paper is likewife ufed for filtring; and
that

that now employed for that purpofe is the common blotting paper, which is very tender, the publick are therefore herewith informed that this inconvenience is like-wife remedied, and at the Neckinger-mill is now manufacturing a paper, fuperior to any other, in ftrength and durability, for the purpofe of filtring, and fold by the bundle, or two reams, for a moderate price; which paper has been examined, tried, and approved of by Dr. Crichton and other experienced chymifts.

I finifh now thefe accounts and obfer-vations which I thought proper to add to this work, and I proceed with the hiftorical account of the fubftances which have been ufed to defcribe events, and to convey ideas, from the earlieft date to the invention of paper.

In the moft ancient time, when writing was not yet difcovered, very fimple means were

were ufed to preferve the remembrance of
important events. Tradition reprefented,
therefore, during many centuries, what
now is more completely effected by writing and printing. Trees were planted,
heaps of ftone, or unornamented altars and
pillars, were erected, plays and feftivals
were ordered, and fongs fung to keep up
the recollection of paft facts. The facred
hiftory mentions, that the Patriarchs erected
altars or heaps of ftones as remembrances
of paft events.

Rough ftones and ftakes were the firft
reminding letters of the Phœnicians. In
the environs of Cadiz, feveral heaps of
ftones have been found; monuments of
Hercules's expedition againft Spain. The
ancient inhabitants of the North placed,
in different fituations, ftones of an extraordinary large fize, to remember great events.
And we have found, in modern times, that
the favages in America do the fame; and

fome

ſome place bows on the tombs of men, and mortars with peſtles on the tombs of women. It has been likewiſe a cuſtom to give names to certain places, and their environs, which referred to the tranſactions and deeds which there took place.

Since the art of writing was invented, ſeveral materials have been uſed, on which was engraved or written what was wiſhed to be conveyed to poſterity. But nothing poſitive can be aſcertained with reſpect to the different materials employed by the ancients for that purpoſe, except that a diſtinction has been made between public records and private writings. For the firſt; ſtones, timber, and metals, were chiefly uſed; and, for the latter, leaves and bark of trees. The Egyptians, the inhabitants of the Northern countries, and ſeveral others, made uſe of ſtones, rocks, and pillars, for that purpoſe.

Job

Job mentions rocks as the materials ufed in his time; and the Danes engraved like-wife upon rocks the deeds of their anceftors.

Jofephus has related, that the children of Seth had, before the deluge, erected two pillars, and thereupon engraved their inventions and aftronomical difcoveries, the one of which was of ftone, and the other of brick-clay, becaufe they had heard, from their grandfather, Adam, that the world would be deftroyed once by fire, and once by water; and, to prevent their knowledge of the motion of planets, &c. being loft to pofterity, they had engraved it on the before-mentioned pillars, the one of which could not be deftroyed by water, nor the other by fire; and the fame author ftates, that the fame pillar of ftone exifted ftill, in his time, in the country of Siriad. But where that country was fituated is very difficult to afcertain; fome fay in Syria. Marfham, Vofz, and others,

affert

aſſert it to be *Seirath*, mentioned in the Scripture, (*Judges*, chap. iii. ver. 26); the moſt likely ſuppoſition ſeems to be, according to Dodwell, Stillingfleet, and Fabricius, that it was ſituated in Egypt.

Theſe pillars bring into recollection others more celebrated, erected by Bacchus, Hercules, Oſiris, and Seſoſtris, to commemorate their exploits. But the moſt famous were the pillars of Mercury Triſmegiſtus, on which his doctrines and rules were engraved with hieroglyphic characters. Porphyrius mentions ſome pillars in the Iſland of Crete, on which the ſacrificial ſervice of Cybeles, and the religious rites were engraved; and, at the time of Demoſthenes, there was ſtill a column of ſtone exiſting, on which the code of laws was engraved. Numerous other pillars could be mentioned, but it is ſufficiently aſcertained, that the moſt ancient nations were not acquainted with any other method

thod of keeping in remembrance their
code of laws, acts and contracts, the hiftory of events, and important difcoveries;
and thefe public records have been the
fources of knowledge of the ancient authors.

It was likewife a cuftom to write on
bricks, and ftone plates, principally to
immortalize laws, inftitutions, and important events.

The Babylonians, according to Pliny,
wrote their firft aftronomical obfervations
on bricks, and the Oftracifm* of the Athenians

---

* The *Oftracifm* was invented by the Athenians
when they became jealous of Ariftides, who at firft
was loved and refpected, and received for his furname
the Juft. But elevated with victories, they thought
themfelves capable of every thing, and were uneafy
to fee a fellow-citizen raifed to fuch extraordinary
honour and diftinction; they affembled at Athens
from all towns in Attica, and banifhed Ariftides by
the Oftracifm; difguifing their envy of his character
under

nians was sometimes inscribed on oister-
shells,

under the specious pretence of guarding against tyranny.
The Ostracism was conducted in the following manner:
every citizen took a piece of a broken pot, or a shell, on
which he wrote the name of the person he wanted to
have banished, and carried it to a part of the market-
place that was enclosed with wooden rails; the magis-
trates then counted the number of the shells, and pieces
of broken pots; and if it did not amount to six thousand, the Ostracism stood for nothing; if it did, they
sorted them, and the person whose name was found on
the greatest number, was declared an exile for ten years,
but with permission to enjoy his estate.

At the time that Aristides was banished, when the
people were inscribing the names on the shells, and pieces
of broken pots, it is reported that an illiterate burgher
came to Aristides, whom he took for some ordinary
person, and giving him his shell, desired him to write
Aristides upon it. The good man, surprised at the
adventure, asked him " Whether Aristides had ever
" injured him?" " No," said he; " nor do I even
" know him; but it vexes me to hear him constantly
" praised, and every where called *the Just.*" Aristides made no answer, but took the shell; and having
written his own name upon it, returned it to the man.
Thus was the man rewarded who was the deliverer of
Athens, and had by uprightness and justice so greatly
contributed to its happiness, When he quitted Athens,
he lifted up his hands towards heaven, and, agreeably
to his character, made a prayer different from that of
Achilles,

ſhells, and in general on the fragments of broken pots.

The moſt ancient monuments of Chineſe knowledge were engraved on hard and large ſtones. The ten commandments were written on ſtone or marble plates; which ſeems more likely than as is ſuppoſed by ſome fanciful writers, who, to dignify thoſe tables, hold out, that they were made of precious ſtones, rubies, carbuncles, or amethyſts; but as nothing of this appears in the ſacred original, it is more probable that they were of ſuch
ſtones

Achilles, namely, " That the people of Athens might " never ſee the day which ſhould force them to remem- " ber Ariſtides." Three years after, the Athenians reverſed this decree, and by a public ordinance recalled all the exiles. The principal inducement was their fear of Ariſtides; for they were apprehenſive that he might join the enemy, corrupt great part of the citizens, and draw them over to the intereſt of the enemy. But they little knew the worthy man; for, before this ordinance of theirs, he had been exciting and encouraging the Greeks to defend their liberty.

ſtones as were found at the ſpot, which
might be moſt likely marble, being abundant in Egypt, and which were hewn,
and poliſhed, by the hand, or direction of
Moſes. Joſhua wrote the other laws on
plates of the ſame kind, and the names
of the twelve Jewiſh tribes were carved
on precious ſtones on the ephod of the
high prieſt. The inſcriptions on Mount
Sinai, and the ſurrounding mountains, ought
to be noticed here, if their antiquity could
be aſcertained. The hieroglyphics of the
Egyptians, who boaſted to be the moſt
ancient of all nations, are chiefly found
on obeliſks, ſtone pillars, &c. and the de-
crees of Lycurgus were carved in ſtone.
A very ancient Grecian ſuperſcription on
ſtone is exiſting on the weſt borders of
Aſia Minor, where the Mitylenians have
built the city of Sigium, from the gathered ſtones of the city of Troy. This
city was deſtroyed long ago by the Ilien-
ſians; the ſtone ſtill lies in the village of
Ieni-

Ieni-Hiffary, called, by the Turks, Gaurkioi,
before the porch of the Greek church,
and is ufed for a feat. The infcription on
this ftone is now upwards of 2360 years
old. William Sherard, Efq. Britifh Conful
at Smyrna, took the firft copy of it; and
Samuel Lifle, preacher to the Englifh re-
fiding at Smyrna, copied it carefully, and
it was afterwards engraved and printed in
London, on nine fheets, by his Majefty's
chaplain, Edmund Chifhull, with explanations, in the year 1721. Still more ancient
infcriptions at Amyclae, have been
difcovered, and publifhed by Fourmont
and Barthemely. They are written
in the fame manner as thofe of Sigeum,
refembling plough-furrows, but they go
from the right to the left, and were
preferved in the Royal Cabinet, at Paris.
Numerous other ancient infcriptions on
ftone are found commemorated in Carften
Niebuhr's Travels in Arabia. The conven-
tion of the Smyrnans and Magnefians was
engraved

engraved on marble 270 years before
the birth of Chrift, and the *Jus Publicum*
of the Athenians was engraved on triangular ftones named Cyrbes. Numerous
old infcriptions in the Etrufcan, Greek,
and Latin languages, on ftone and marble,
on plates, urns, vafes, and farcophagi,
are ftill preferved in the firft and feventh
room of the gallery of the Grand Duke of
Tufcany at Florence; and in the firft room of
that gallery are feveral infcriptions on burnt
clay, with which the Etrufcans covered
the unburnt bodies of their deceafed friends.
The Latin incriptions are divided into twelve
claffes. The firft thereof commences with
the gods, and their priefts. In each of them
are preferved fome of thofe which have
been brought from Africa by Pagni,
defcribed by Gori, Falconieri, and Spon;
they are diftinguifhed by the Greek λ
which is ufed in the place of the Latin I.
The fecond clafs relates to the Emperors,
and contains amongft others the fo much
admired

admired bafes by Maffei, and a large epifty-
lium which is faftened in the wall above
the principal door. It was found with four
others at Civita Vecchia in a dark repofitory
belonging to monuments facred to Tiberius
and Livia. It is worth the notice of antiquarians, that on this marble after the name
of Tiberius fome of the infcription has been
erafed, and replaced with the words DIVAE
AUGUSTAE, which may be occafioned by
Claudius's adoration of Livia. The third
clafs refers to the confuls and other
Romans of rank. The fourth, to the Roman municipalities, to which have been
added a great many, new and beautiful.
The fifth, for the publick buildings and
plays in which the mile-pillars are in-
included. The fixth, for the military.
The feventh, and eighth, contain the titles
given by furviving relations to their
deceafed anceftors. The ninth, relates
to flaves who got their freedom. The
tenth contains monuments of chriftianity.
The

The eleventh, such inscriptions of only the names of deceased persons. And the twelfth is a mixture of different inscriptions, amongst whom many are doubtful and seem to be counterfeited. But Maffei in his *Arte critica lapidaria*, recommends notwithstanding the preservation of these inscriptions, because they may serve for publick information, and principally, that at one time or the other it may be proved, they are genuine, as has been the case with the inscription of Scipio Barbatus, and several others in the collection of Riccardi, which were declared by Maffei, to be counterfeit. But notwithstanding several of them have been proved to be counterfeit, by the colour of the marble, the most part are genuine, which satisfactorily proves the art of writing was known to the ancients.

But these materials were soon found to be difficult to write upon, and therefore others, more simple and more convenient, were

were fought for. Bricks and ftones were
changed for different kinds of metals, and
lead became then the moft ancient writing
fubftance. Job mentions, in chapter xix.
verfe 24, engravings with an iron pen
on lead; and Paufanias fays, that Hefiod's
Opera et Dies was written on leaden tables,
which were preferved on the mountain of
Helicon. Pliny ftates, that lead was ufed
for writing, which was rolled up like a
cylinder. Hirtius wrote to Decius Brutus
on leaden tables. In Italy were preferved
two documents of Pope Leo III. and
Luitbrand, King of the Longobards; and,
according to Kircher's Mufeum, table X.
many more of fuch writings on lead are
to be found. For example, Montfaucon
notices a very ancient book of eight leaden
leaves, the firft and laft was ufed as a
cover, and that it contains numerous myf-
terious figures of the Bafilidians, and words
partly Greek, and partly of Etrufcan letters. On the back were rings faftened, by

H   means

means of a fmall leaden rod, to keep them together. Paufanias notices likewife, in his Meffenica, that Epiteles dug up out of the earth a brafs veffel, or urn, which he carried to Epaminondas, (about 350 or 360 years before the birth of Chrift,) in which there was a fine plate of lead or tin, rolled up in the form of a book, on which were written the rites and ceremonies of the great goddeffes. And we have a late difcovery of writing on lead, if the account given in the Gentleman's Magazine, July 1757, may be depended on; it is no longer ago than in the year 304. " In a ftone cheft, the acts of the council of Illiberis, held anno 304, were found at Granada in Spain; they are written or engraved on plates of lead, in Gothic characters, and are now tranflating into Spanifh."

Bronze was afterwards more frequently ufed than lead, as is certified in the Hiftory

tory of the Maccabees, by Dionyfius of Halicarnaffus, Cicero, Livy, Pliny, Suetonius, and Julius Obfequens. Phœnician letters were on the kettle of bronze, devoted by Cadmus to Minerva, who was adored at Lindus, on the ifland of Rhodes. But, as the kettle is not only loft, and the copies of the infcription, with thofe of Cadmifian letters, on feveral tripod veffels, mentioned by Herodotus, and others, I fhall confine myfelf to thofe which ftill exift, of which the moft remarkable are the famous *Scriptum de Bachanalibus*, in the Imperial Library; Trajan's *Tabula Alimentaria;* and the helmet, found at Cannae, with Punic letters, defcribed in the *Mufeo Etrufco* of Gori, and which is now in the third room of the gallery of the Grand Duke of Tuf-cany, at Florence. I cannot omit noticing the eight tables of bronze, found in the town of Gubbio, in a fubterraneous cabinet, when, in the year 1444, parts of an amphi-theatre were removed: on feven tables the

infcriptions

infcriptions were in the Latin, and one in the Etrufcan language. Since that time feveral bronze tables, with Etrufcan writing, have been dug up in Tufcany. The feven Latin have been defcribed and engraved on copper-plates, by Merula, Gruter, and others, and one by Thomas Demfter.

The criminal, civil, and ceremonial laws of the Greeks have been engraved on bronze tables, and the fpeech of Claudius, engraved on plates of bronze, are yet preferved at the town-hall of Lyons, in France.

The celebrated ftatutes or laws on twelve tables, the major part of which the Romans copied from the Grecian code, were firft written on tables of oak, but according to others on ten ivory tables, and hung up *pro roftris.* But, after they had been approved by the people, they were engraved in bronze. But thefe were melted through fire occafioned by lightning which

ftruck

ftruck the capitolium, and confumed likewife numerous other laws for the cities and
country, which were there depofited; the
lofs thereof was highly regretted by the
Emperor Octavius Auguftus. The laws of
the Cretans were likewife engraved in
bronze; and the Romans etched, in general, their code *plebifcita*, contracts, conven-
tions, and public records, in brafs, not
only during the exiftence of the republic,
but likewife under the reign of the Emperors. The magiftrates of Athens were
chofen by lot; the names of the candidates
were written on bronze plates, and put into
an urn, with white and black beans, and
the perfon whofe name was taken out with
a white bean was elected.

The pacts between the Romans, Spartans,
and the Jews, were written on brafs, which
method was likewife obferved by the guilds
and private perfons who ufually, for fecu-
rity, got the land-marks of their eftates

H 3   engraved

engraved on metal; and in many cabinets
are yet to be feen the difcharges of foldiers
written on copper-plates. It is not long
fince, at Mongheer, in Bengal, a copper-
plate was dug up, on which characters of
Schanfcreet were etched fignifying a gift
of land, from Bideram Gunt Raja of Bengal, to one of his fubjects. This bill of
feoffment, on copper, is dated 100 years
before the birth of Chrift, and proves at
the fame time that the Indians were,
about two thoufand years ago, in a high
degree of cultivation. Such genuine documents, written on fuch hard fubftances, in
more modern times are very fcarce. The
Archbifhop Adelbert, of Mentz, ordered
a grant to be engraved on metal plates,
which privilege is kept over the door-wings
of the church B. *Mariæ Virginis ad gradus,*
in Mentz; and, in 1011, thefe door-wings
were manufactured of caft metal, refembling bronze, by the Archbifhop Willigis.

The

The Abbot Cabent, and the Benedictine Monk Legipont, entertain the opinion, that the most ancient writing material which has been used was wood. It is certain that box-wood, deals, and ivory tables, have in those times been occasionally made use of to write upon, but of the precise time nothing can be ascertained with certainty.

Isaiah (chapter xxx. verse 8), and Habakkuk (chapter ii. verse 2), make mention of writings upon tables, that it may be remembered for the time to come, for ever and ever.* Solon's Civil Laws were written on boards, which were placed in a machine,

---

* Solomon, in the Book of Proverbs, (chap. iii. ver. 3.) in allusion to this way of writing on thin slices of wood, advises his son, to *write his precepts upon the table of his heart.* Solomon lived about one thousand years before the birth of Christ, and Habakkuk near four hundred years later; between which two different periods, different authors place the birth of Homer. This proves, that the *pugillares,* or tables of wood to write on, were in use before Homer's time, but how long before, no authentic account can be obtained.

a machine, conftructed to turn them eafily, called *axones;* and, even in the fourth century, the laws of the Emperors were publifhed on wooden tables, painted with cerufe, which gave rife to the expreffion in Horace: *Leges incidere ligno.* The Swedes had the fame cuftom, for which reafon the laws are ftill by them named, *Balkar,* originating from a piece of timber, called *Balkan,* which is a balk or beam.

The Greeks and Romans ufed commonly, at an early period, either plain wooden boards or covered with wax. The Greeks called wooden boards which were not covered with wax, *Schedæ* or *Schedulæ.* On fuch *Schedulas* was written, in the Hebrew language, the Gofpel of Matthew, which, according to Baronius, in his *Martyrologium Romanum,* was found in the tomb of the Apoftle Barnabas. The name of *pugillares* given by the ancient Romans, originates from *pugillum,* becaufe they could

could be held in one hand; thefe tablets alfo were fometimes called *codices* and *codicilli*; from *caudes*, the trunk of a tree, being cut into thin flices, and finely planed, and polifhed; and they ufually confifted of two, three, five, and fometimes of more leaves; from whence they were more diftinguifhingly denominated by the Greeks *diptycha*, *triptycha*, and *pentaptycha*; and thofe leaves, being waxed over, or overlaid with wax, were named *Pugillaris cerei*, and were written upon, with an inftrument called a ftile. Yet it is very probable, that thofe tablets, being only thin flices of wood, having a fmooth furface, were at firft written upon juft as they were planed; and that the overlaying them with wax, was an improvement of that invention. Perfons who would privately correfpond, or give fecret intelligence to others, wrote it on plain wooden boards, on which they laid wax after they had written on the wood. Pliny affures us, that the writing on wooden

boards

boards was a cuftom even before the Trojan war. Such boards have been fometimes fimply named *Cera*, from which originate the defcription *Cera prima*, *Cera fecunda*, *Cera tertia*, &c. which fignifies the firft fecond, and third page. The ancient Jurifts unite often the words *Tabulæ* and *Cerae*. It appears notwithftanding, that they defcribe under the denomination of *Tabulis*, a carefully written work, and under that of *Ceris* and *Pugillaribus*, they comprehend a carelefs written manufcript, or copy of writing. Numerous teftaments have been made on *Tabulas ceratas*. But I recommend attention to the ftated boards or tables, to prevent mifreprefentation; be-caufe, under the general defcription of *Tabulæ*, is often underftood not only wooden boards, but alfo ftone, ivory, and metal tables and plates.

The Romans employed for common ufe, and principally for writing letters, fmall boards

boards of common wood, overlaid with
bees wax, which were fealed in linen
clothes; and, if the laft will was written
upon thefe boards, they were run through,
and joined together with lace or tape.
They ufed likewife very thin levelled
boards, of foft wood, named, according to
Martial, *Tenues tabellas,* which were not
overlaid with wax, but in which the
letters were carved.

In the archives of the town-hall in
Hanover, are kept twelve wooden boards,
overlaid with bees wax, on which are
written the male and female names of
owners of houfes, and of houfes without
noticing the ftreets; but, as Hanover was
divided, in 1428, into ftreets, we have
reafon to believe, that thefe wooden manufcripts are more ancient. Thefe boards
are apparently of beech wood, and have
on the four corners an elevation, and the
places within are filled up with green
wax.

wax. The firſt and laſt table ſerve, at the
ſame time, as a cover, and are, therefore,
only on one ſide overlaid with wax, but the
others on both ſides. Theſe twelve boards
form therefore only twenty-two pages; the
outſide boards are joined by a piece of
leather paſted on them, to form the back
of the book, and the leather is faſtened,
by nails, to the other ten boards. This
curious manuſcript book is one foot five
inches high, eight and an half inches wide,
and about five and an half inches thick,
or each leaf about half an inch. There
is, beſides the before-mentioned elevation
on the four corners, another croſs elevation, which divides every ſheet into four
ſquare columns: on each page are between
ſixty and ſeventy lines of Monkiſh letters,
which are apparently preſſed in the wax
with a feſcue. Seven pages are in good
preſervation. Another manuſcript, much
like this, is in the gallery at Florence, in
the third room in the eleventh ſcrine;

another

another in the city library of Geneva; and
feveral are ftill exifting in other libraries
and archives, of which I only will notice
the wooden Runen-almanack; and the
waxed boards which are, according to
Lewis of Strafbourgh, ftill preferved in the
church of the Salines at Halle.

The rich Romans ufed, inftead of wooden
boards overlaid with bees wax, thin pieces
of ivory, named *libri eborei*, or *libri ele-*
phantini; and Ulpian ftates, that the principal tranfactions of great princes have
been ufually written with a black colour
on ivory. Flavias Vopifcus fays, that there
was a book of ivory in the library of
Ulpian. The exiftence of ivory books has
been fully afcertained by Martial, Salma-
fius, and Schwarz, notwithftanding other
authors have held out, that the name of
libri elephantini originates from the enormous fize of thefe books, or from the
inteftines of elephants, on which they
have

have been written; but this is certain, that
only the great and the rich were able to
ufe ivory tables, becaufe they were fcarce
and dear.

It muft be obferved, that thefe wooden
tables overlaid with wax were of different
fizes; and, according to Quintilian, likewife ufed to teach writing to beginners;
and, according to Cicero, it feems that the
critics were accuftomed by reading wax
manufcripts to notice obfcure or wrong
phrafes, by joining a piece of red wax.
The Greeks and Romans continued ftill to
make ufe of fuch boards, even at the time
when writing on leaves of trees, on Egyptian Paper, on membranous fubftances,
and on parchment, was already adopted,
becaufe they could thereupon put down
their fugitive ideas, and change or correct
them eafily, before they wrote on other
fubftances; and it has been proved, that
even when linen Paper was firft difcovered,

fuch

fuch boards have been fometimes made ufe of. The Chinefe have, in very ancient times, likewife written with large iron tools on boards, pieces of bamboo, and occafionally on metal.

Curious refearchers are recommended to confult Perizonius's inftructive notes upon the 12th chapter of the 14th book of Aelian's Various Hiftory, where we are informed alfo, that thefe wooden table-books were often made of the linden or lime-tree, as well as of box, to which the maple may be likewife added, which, being capable of an elegant polifh, was ufed for the fame purpofe. Thus Ovid fays,

—————— *Veneri fidas fibi Nafo Tabellas*
Dedicat, at nuper vile fuiftis Acer.

—————— This trufty table-book,
To thee, O Venus, now I dedicate,
Which was but worthlefs maple-wood of late.

But

But box was neverthelefs commonly ufed, and we may judge of the ornaments of thofe wooden books from the following diftich in Propertius.

Non * illas fixum caras effecerat aurum,
Vulgari buxo fordida cera fuit.

With gold my tablets were not coftly made,
On common box the fordid wax was laid.

The ufe of boards was fuperfeded by the ufe of the leaves of palm, olive, poplar, and other trees. According to Pliny, the Egyptians were the firft who wrote on palm leaves, for which reafon their letters obtained the name of Phœnixcian letters, becaufe the Greeks called the palm-tree *Phœnix.* In the library of the city of Strahlfund is a book ftill to be feen, written on palm leaves. The Malabars yet write on leaves of the palm, *Corypha umbra culifera,* and form the letters with a fefcue at leaft twelve inches long, and anoint the

leaves

* *Tabellas.*

leaves afterwards with oil. The written letters are rolled up. Their books are of many fuch leaves, which are joined toge-ther with a tape, and framed between two thin boards of the fame fize. There are Bibles ftill preferved, written on fuch leaves; one of them, the Telugian or Warugian Bible, is to be feen in the library of the univerfity of Gottingen, containing 5376 leaves, formed into forty-five fheets, which has been purchafed from Baum-garten, in a public fale; another is at Copenhagen; and one in the Orphan's houfe, at Halle; which are all the copies of this fcarce work to be found in Eu-rope; but that preferved at Halle is, ac-cording to Dreyhaupt, not written in the Telugian, but in the Damulian language. The explanation of twelve large volumes, with plants of Malabar, to be feen in the Academical Mufeum at Gottingen, is moftly drawn with a fefcue on palm leaves. In Heffelberg's library, at Copenhagen, was a

I   part

part of the New Teftament, written in the Malabar language, on palm leaves. The Bramin manufcript, in the Kulingiennian language, which was fent from Fort St. George to Oxford, is of Malabar palm leaves; and Mr. Aftle ftates, in his Origin and Progrefs of Writing, (chapter iv. page 49,) that in Sir Hans Sloane's library were more than twenty manufcripts of palm leaves, written in different Afiatic languages; and he fays, (chapter viii. page 203,) that he himfelf is in poffeffion of a manufcript, written on palm leaves, in the Peguan language, which is twenty-one inches long, and three inches and an half wide ; the ground of which is richly ornamented with gold, and the letters are inlaid with a black gummy-like fubftance.

Knox ftates, in his Hiftory of Ceylon, that there grows a kind of palm tree, of which the leaves are woolly, and of con-fiderable breadth, named the pananga tree, which

which are ufed by the inhabitants for writing, after having taken off the outer fkin.
They ufe talipot-tree leaves for the fame
purpofe.

Pliny, who was a diligent enquirer into
antiquity, fays, fpeaking particularly of
the Egyptians, that they wrote upon the
leaves of palm trees; or, according to the
various reading of *malvarum* for *palmarum*,
upon the leaves of mallows. But it is probable, the ancients wrote upon any leaves
that they could make fit for that purpofe.
Hoffman, in his Lexicon, under the word
palma, ftates, from Petrus de la Valle, that
the Indian Brachmans write upon the
leaves of palm trees, and that one of
them made him a prefent of a book
compofed of thefe leaves. It was likewife the cuftom of the Sibyls of old to
write their prophecies upon leaves, as
appears by the following lines in Virgil,
(Æneid, lib. iii. v. 443.)

I 2   A raging

A raging prophetefs you there fhall fee,
Who from her cave fings what the fates decree;
Her myftic numbers writes on leaves, and then
In order lays, and lurks within her den;
Before the door they lie, as they were plac'd,
But if that opening, or fome fudden blaft
Should them diforder, fhe no more will fing,
Nor when once fcatter'd, to contexture bring.

This ufage of the Sibyls writing upon leaves
was fo current, that it became proverbial
among the Romans to ufe *folium Sibyllae*
for any undoubted truth. Thus Juvenal
fays,

Credite me vobis folium recitare Sibyllae.

Believe me, what I here declare to you,
Is truth itfelf; no Sibyls leaf more true.

The fentence of banifhment or *pedalifm*
(petalifmus) of the Syracufans, according to
Diodorus Siculus, was written on olive-tree
leaves; and on the fame kind of leaves
were written the names of thofe who were
excluded from the Senate of Athens, which
punifhment was called *Ekphyllophorefis.*

The

The East Indians have, and still use, in some parts, leaves for writing. And, according to Helvetius Cinna, poplar-tree leaves have been likewise used.

The inhabitants of the Maldivia islands write on leaves of the macarcquo tree, which are three fathoms long, and one foot wide; and sometimes on thin wooden boards after they have been painted white. In many places in the East Indies, the leaves of the musa or banana tree were used for writing, till the Europeans introduced paper; and in the island of Java they still write on the leaves of the lantor tree, which are very smooth, and five or six feet long. Several other eastern nations use, for that purpose, the leaves of the cocoa tree, the taon-condar tree, and of a tree named, by the Malays, olen, which grows every where plentifully in that country, and is a kind of wild palm tree, the leaves of which are about one yard and

an

an half long, and three inches wide; for extensive writings they are tied together. The letters are written thereon with an iron tool, which pierces the outside covering, and makes indelible letters, which method is preferred by the Indians, because they are ruled by the touch and not by the eye: those leaves have a quality which makes them preferable to our paper; they are not only very strong, but, if they remain even for a long time in water, they are not liable to rot or grow tender, and the writing is not destroyed, for which reason the natives continued to use them, notwithstanding many paper-mills have been erected in India. It is remarkable, that poplar-tree leaves were principally used for sacred writings, which may be the reason why Pythagoras calls the leaf of the poplar-tree, a sacred leaf.

The custom of writing on leaves of trees was superseded by the use of the raw bark

of

of trees, and the interior bark of the lime
tree, of which Suidas remarks, that it refembles *Papyrus*; and alfo the bark of
elder, elm, and birch tree. The exterior
bark (*cortex*) was feldom ufed, being too
coarfe in general, and not fufficiently
fmooth to write on legibly and eafily.
The interior bark (*liber*) was therefore preferred, being fmooth and fine. From this
originates the Latin name for a book. To
carry thofe barks commodioufly in the
pocket, they were rolled up, and called
volumen; which name has been continued
for rolls of paper and parchment, and for
books, notwithftanding our books have a
a very different fhape. The name *codex*,
or more properly *caudex*, ftill in ufe, originates in a like manner: and notwith
ftanding its true meaning is the trunk of a
tree, it was adopted to defcribe many
fheets of the faid bark-fhavings together.

The fhape of the bark-fhavings on which

I 4   the

the ancient Europeans wrote was not all of
the fame fize, and thofe manufcripts are
very fcarce. Montfaucon fays that there
are none in Italy, and that he found only
one in the archives of the city of St. Denis,
in France. Cragus faw in the city of Chur,
in Switzerland, fome verfes of Virgil written
on the interior bark of the birch tree. It
is ftated in *Acta Petropolitana,* tom x.
page 449, that many whole books of this
kind have been found in Siberia, the letters
of which were in the language of the
Calmuks. The ancient favorite fong: *Eija
mit hierta ratt innerlig,* &c. was called the
Birch fong, becaufe Elfa, the daughter of
Andres, had originally written it on the
bark of a birch tree. The protocols of
the Emperors were in thefe times written
on the fame writing-material to prevent
falfifying, becaufe, if the furface was
fhaved in the fmalleft degree, the letters
were deftroyed, and could not be replaced
by others. Several nations ufe it ftill for
writing,

writing, notwithftanding paper is well
known to them. Mr. von Jufti afferts
that he poffeffes a letter written, in the
Malabar language, on the bark of a tree;
and the Orphan-houfe at Halle, in Germany, poffeffes likewife a large manufcript
with Bomanian letters. In Sir Hans Sloane's
library, was a manufcript written in Patta-
nian charaĉters; and a letter of a Nabob,
two yards long, richly ornamented with
gold. In the Britifh Mufeum are feveral
pieces of the exterior and interior bark of
trees, written on; and many more are in
other Britifh libraries. In the gallery of
the Grand Duke of Tufcany, at Florence,
in the third apartment and the eleventh
partition, are feveral writings on bark, but
not ancient: but of the antiquity of a very
great number of the like manufcripts in
the Vatican library, in Greek, Hebrew,
Arabic, and Latin, there is not the leaft
doubt.

To

To this fucceeded the method of painting the letters with pencils, on linen and
cotton:—whether thefe cloths were of the
fame kind as thofe now in ufe, cannot be
afcertained. According to Symmachius, a
great many of the prophecies of the Sybils
were likewife written on linen cloth. And
Livy ftates the fame, of the annual regifters
of the Romans. But Pliny fays, linen
was only ufed for writing in private affairs,
notwithftanding, Livy and Claudian, and
the Theodofian Codex have proved the
contrary; and in the latter (tit. xxvii.
cap. 11.) is principally noticed a law, written
on *mappas linteas.* The Chinefe wrote two
thoufand years ago, in the reign of Tfin,
before they invented the art of making
paper, on pieces of linen or filk, cut to fuch
a fize as they wifhed to have the book.
But it was not ufual for the Greeks to write
on linen. Count Caylus remarks, that there
were found, fometimes in the boxes containing Egyptian mummies, very neat cha-
characters

characters, written on linen. It feems natural,
that all linen, ufed for writing, muft have
been fteeped in fize or gum, or the ink
and paint muft have blotted.

Of the inhabitants of Partha, it is faid
that they wrote upon the fame ftuff of
which they made clothes. And fome
Indians write yet on a kind of cloth, named
Syndon.

But, as linen was too much fubjeɛt to
become mouldy, animals were then
attacked, to furnifh ftuff for a writing
material:—their fkins (*coria*) were principally ufed to write upon, after they had
been tanned on both fides: thofe of fheep,
goats, and affes were preferred. Several
books, written on thefe, were in the Vatican
library; in that of the King of France; and
in feveral others. In the convent of the
Dominican monks at Bologna, are two
books of Efdras, written on affes fkins, which

are

are faid to be the original manufcripts of
Efdras himfelf: but it is certain that it
has been written only about five hundred
years ago, and it looks like leather. This
copy was given to the Prior Aymerico,
of that convent, by a Jew, in the commencement of the fourteenth century, who
by this bribe endeavoured to fecure his
fellow Jews againft the Inquifition, and
therefore to make it the more precious
and valuable affured the Prior it was the
genuine hand-writing of Ezra.

The ancient Perfians and Ionians wrote
on hides from which the hair was fcraped
And the fhepherds in former times wrote
their fongs with thorns and awls on ftraps
of leather, which they wound round their
crooks.

The Icelanders fcratched their *runes,* a
kind of figurative writing, or hieroglyphic,
fometimes on walls: and it is noticed in
the

the *Laxdaela Saga*, that Olof, at Hiardar-
hult, has built a large houfe, on the balks
and fpars of which he has got engraved the
hiftory of his own and more ancient times:
and Thorkil Hake wrote his own deeds, in
thofe hieroglyphics, on his chair and bed.
The most ancient *runes* are traced to the
third century; and the most ancient hif-
torian, who mentioned them, is Venantius
Fortunatus, who lived in the fixth century.*
Of thefe letters, or hieroglyphics, there
were no more than fixteen in the whole;
but as, in the year one thoufand, the Chriftian faith was introduced into Iceland, they
were found infufficient, and Latin letters
were adopted.

Puricelli maintains, that the Italian
Kings, Hugo and Lotharis, had given a
grant to the Ambrofian church, at Milan,
written on the fkin of a fifh, which
Muratori

* He fays in Carm. vii. 18, Barbara fraxineis pingatur
Runa tabellis.

Muratori took for a kind of parchment by the want of fufficient inveftigation.

Not only the fkins of animals were ufed for a writing fubftance, but alfo bones and entrails, if they were thought to be fit for that purpofe. In the hiftory of Mahomet, is flightly noticed, that the Arabians took the fhoulder-bones of fheep, on which they carved remarkable events with a knife; and, after tying them with a ftring, they hung their chronicle up in their cabinets.

In the library of the Egyptian King Ptolomœus Philadelphus, which is faid to have contained 700,000 volumes, were the works of Homer, written in golden letters on the fkins of ferpents and other animals; and under the reign of the Emperor Bafilifkus, was burned, at Conftantinople, a manufcript one hundred and twenty feet long, written on the inteftines of beafts, &c.

in

in golden letters, containing Homer's Iliad
and Odyſſey. In the library of the Emperor Zeno Iſauricus were likewiſe Homer's
works, painted in golden letters on the
entrails of animals: and we know, from
Iſodorus, that the inteſtines of elephants
have been alſo uſed for writing.

But theſe writing-materials were neither
common writing-maſſes nor in general uſe,
and regarded rather as a rarity. There is
in his Majeſty's library at Hanover a letter
engraved on a golden plate, written by
an independant prince of the coaſt of Co-
romandel to King George the Second which
is about three feet long and four inches wide,
and inlaid on both of the narrow ſides with
diamonds, which was delivered to the late
Mr. Scheidt, to be there kept.

We arrive now at the period when the
Egyptian Paper was invented, and manufactured from the rind of the Paper-plant,
                                    Papyrus,

*Papyrus,** which grows in the marfhes on the borders of the Nile, and is called in the Egyptian language *Berd*, or *al Berdi*. Theophraftus, Pliny, Guilandin, Profper Alpin, and other authors, defcribe the Egyptian

* The Egyptians call it *Berd*, and they eat that part of the plant which is near the roots. The internal part of the bark of this plant was made into paper; and the manner of the manufacture was as follows: Strips, or leaves of every length that could be obtained, being laid upon a table, other ftrips were placed acrofs, and pafted to them by the means of water and a prefs, fo that this paper was a texture of feveral ftrips; and it even appears that, in the time of the Emperor Claudius, the Romans made paper of three lays. Pliny alfo fays, that the leaves of the *Papyrus* were fuffered to dry in the fun, and afterwards diftributed according to their different qualities fit for different kind of paper; fcarce more than twenty ftrips could be feparated from each ftalk. This paper never exceeded thirteen fingers breadth. In order to be deemed perfeft, it was to be thin, com-paft, white, and fmooth. It was fleeked with a tooth, and this kept it from foaking the ink, and made it glifter. It received an agglutination, which was pre-pared with flour of wheat, diluted with boiling water, on which were thrown fome drops of vinegar; or with crumbs of leavened bread, diluted with boiling water, and paffed through a bolting cloth. Being afterwards beaten with a hammer, it was fized a fecond time, put to the prefs, and extended with the hammer.

Egyptian Paper-reed to be a plant of the rufh
kind, which grows in fwamps about ten
cubits long. The ftalk is triangular, and
of a thicknefs to be fpanned; its root
crooked; furrounded, near the root, with
fhort leaves, but naked on the ftalk. This
ftalk has on the top a bufh, which refembles in fome refpects a head with hairs,
or of long, thin, ftraight fibres; the root
is brown. After Pliny, Guilandin furnifhes
us with the beft defcription of the *Papyrus;*
and the method how it is prepared for the
ufe of writing; all other fubfequent authors
have, more or lefs, copied them.

The Egyptian Paper-reed which according to Strabo grows only in Egypt and
India, and of which in the year feventy-
nine, after the birth of Chrift, a fpecies
was found in the Euphrates near Babylon,
which was equal in quality to the genuine
Egyptian *Papyrus* for making Paper, muft
not be miftaken, as Ray and others did, for

the

the Papero-plant growing in Sicily, which much refembles the other. Lobel has given a defcription of the Sicilian Papero, in his *Adverfariis*, and it does not feem that it has been ufed in ancient time for making Paper: it is only lately that the Chevalier Savario Landolina has fent famples of Paper to the fociety at Gottingen, manufactured from this plant, according to the defcription which Pliny has given of the manufacture of *Papyrus*.

Many authors believe that the Egyptian Paper-plant is no more exifting, which does not feem likely, becaufe it was a plant in many refpects of the rufh kind; but by the changes which the foil in that country has experienced, it may have become fcarcer. Neverthelefs, it is not noticed by Pocock; and Shaw notices it only amongft the hieroglyphics of the ancient Egyptians. Maillet obferves (which feems to be improbable), *Je ferais cependant affez*

porté

porté à croire, que ce n'eſt autre choſe que la plante appellée au Caire figuier d'Adam, *et par les Arabes* Mons. Moſt of the modern geographers, who deſcribe Egypt, take no notice of this plant, which may lead us to believe that they have either no knowledge thereof, or thought it no objeƈt of conſe-quence, but not that it exiſts no longer: and, as Pliny ſtates that *Papyrus* was not only uſed for making Paper, but for nu-merous other purpoſes, which he deſ-cribes, we muſt preſume that care would have been taken to preſerve ſuch an uſeful plant.

The Egyptian Paper was manufaƈtured from the fine pellicles of the *Papyrus* which ſurrounded the trunk (the fineſt of which were in the middle), and not from the marrow of the plant. Theſe pellicles were ſeparated by means of a pin, or pointed muſcle-ſhells, and ſpread on a table ſprinkled with Nile water, in ſuch a form

as

as the fize of the sheets required, and washed over with hot glue-like Nile-water. On the first layer of these skins, a second was laid crofs-wife to finish the sheet, *(Plagula)* which was preffed, hung up to dry, and fmoothed and polished with a tooth. The Nile-water was laid on with great care, to prevent fpots in the Paper. Twenty skins were the utmoft which could be feparated from one ftalk, and thofe neareft to the pith made the fineft Paper.

Twenty sheets, glued together, were called *fcapus,* but fometimes feveral *fcapi* were glued together, to form a large *volumen.* This part of the bufinefs was executed by the *Glutinatoris,* the work of whom refembles in many refpects that of the bookbinders in our time. All perfons who worked in thefe Paper-manufactures had names according to their work.

With refpect to the time when this
Paper

Paper was invented there are different opinions; and even the name of the inventor
is unknown. Some authors have tried to
prove its antiquity from Homer, Hefiod,
and Herodotus, and conjectured that Mofes
had written his books on Egyptian Paper,
whereas Varro ftates that the invention was
not known in the time of Alexander the
Great, which is about four hundred years
before the birth of Chrift; but as Ariftotle
mentions the book-moths as well-known
infects, it feems likely that the invention
is more ancient; and Pliny refutes Varro,
by quoting Caffius Hemina, who ftates that
a writer named Terentius, by digging
a piece of land on mount Janiculum,
found in a ftone box the books of Numa,
written on Egyptian Paper, which was
completely preferved, notwithftanding it
had been 350 years buried in the earth,
becaufe it had been fteeped in oil of cedar;
and that Mucian, who was three times
conful, had affured him, that during the

time

time he was commander-in-chief in Lycia, he had feen there, in a temple, a letter of the Lycian King, Sarpedon, written on Egyptian Paper. It is true Guilandin has proved that the Paper-reed was known long before the reign of Alexander the Great, which he ftates was ufed for feveral pur-pofes, but thereby cannot be pofitively afcertained that it was ufed as Paper-ftuff.

Neverthelefs, it is remarked by Varro, that foon after the time that Alexander built Alexandria in Egypt, the making paper of the *Papyrus* for writing on, was firft found out in that country. On the invention of which, all the other ways of writing were in a great degree * fuperfeded;

no

---

*This muft be underftood, with fome reftriction; for wooden table-books continued in ufe for ages after. The father of John the Baptift, did not afk for pen, ink, and paper, but a writing-table, to write his name in. Nay, they were common fo late as the fourth century, as appears from the ftory of Caffianus, told by
Prudentius

no materials till then invented being more
convenient to write upon than this. Therefore when Ptolemy Philadelphus, King of
Egypt, began to make a great library,
and to collect all forts of books, he
caufed them to be all copied on this
new invented paper. And it was exported
alfo for the ufe of other countries, till
Eumenes, King of Pergamus, endeavour-
ing to form a library at Pergamus, which
                                                        fhould

---

Prudentius as follows: Caffianus was the firft Bifhop of
Siben in Germany, where he built a church in the year
350. But being banifhed from thence by the infidels,
he fled to Rome; and was afterwards obliged to keep a
publick School for a living at *Forum Cornelii*, now
called *Imola*, an epifcopal city in Italy. But in 365,
he was taken by order of Julian the Apoftate, and expofed to the incenfed cruelty of his fcholars, who killed
him with their *pugillares*, having firft tortured him with
great cruelty with the fame *ftyles*, with which he had
taught them to write. From hence it appears, that fome
of thofe table-books, efpecially fuch as fcholars learned
to write in, were pretty large and heavy. Which is
alfo confirmed by fome lines in Plautus, where he fays,
that a boy of feven years old, broke his mafters head,
with his table-book.

fhould outdo, that at Alexandria, occafioned a prohibition to be put upon the exportation of that commodity; for Ptolemy,
to put a ftop to Eumenes's emulation in this
particular, forbad the carrying any more
paper out of Egypt. This put Eumenes
upon the invention of making paper of
Parchment, and on them he thenceforth
got copied fuch of the works of learned
men, as he afterwards placed in his library; and hence parchment is called
pergamena in Latin, from the City Pergamus, in Leffer-Afia, where it was firft
ufed for this purpofe amongft the Greeks.
But that Eumenes, on this occafion, firft
invented the art of making parchment, is
dubious; for in Ifaiah viii. 1. Jeremiah
xxxvi. 2. Ezekiel ii. 9. and other parts of
the Scriptures, we find mention made of
rolls of writing; and might not thofe rolls
be of parchment? And it is faid by Diodorus Siculus, that the ancient Perfians
wrote all their records on fkins; and
Herodotus

Herodotus tells us of fheep-fkins and goat-
fkins having been made ufe of in writing by
the ancient Iönians many hundred years
before Eumenes's time. It feems therefore poffible, that Eumenes found out a
better way of dreffing them for this ufe
at Pergamus, and perhaps it thenceforth
became the chief trade of the place;
and either of thefe is reafon enough
from *pergamenus* to call them *pergamenæ*.
There is indeed in our Englifh tranflation of Ifaiah's prophecy concerning Egypt,
mention made of paper reeds by the
brooks, (chap. xix. 7.) which prophecy was
delivered four hundred years at leaft before
the time that Varro places the Egyptian
invention; by this one would imagine
that paper made of thofe reeds was in ufe
when that prophecy was written;* for
why

---

* The learned Dr. Gill is of that opinion; for in his
commentary upon the aforefaid verfe in Ifaiah, he fays,
" On the banks of the Nile grew a reed or rufh, called
by the Greeks *papyrus* and *byblus,* from whence come
the

why were they called paper-reeds, if not applied for that purpofe? But little ftrefs can be laid upon this paffage, becaufe the learned are not agreed about the meaning of the original Hebrew word, which is there tranflated paper-reeds. However, let it be the *papyrus*, or let it be *parchment*, that was firft found out to write upon, it is certain that the ufe of parchment has long out-lafted that of the papyrus; for books made of this material are now great curio-fities. Euftathius, in his comment upon the twenty-firft book of Homer's Odyffey, remarks that it was difufed in his time, which is near fix hundred years ago.

The Paper manufactured in Egypt was rather of an inferior quality, and the Romans prepared

---

the word *paper*, and *bible* or book, of which paper was anciently made, even as early as the time of Ifaiah, and fo many hundred years before the time of Alexander the Great, to which time fome fix the æra of making it.

prepared it more carefully, and paid more attention to the wafhing, beating, glueing, fizing, and fmoothing than the Egyptians. They fized it in a fimilar method as we do rag-paper, but they made their fize of the fineft flour, which was ftirred in boiling water with a few drops of vinegar and fome leaven, and then filtered. It was after the firft fize beat with a hammer; fized the fecond time, preffed, and then fmoothed. This Paper of the Romans was very white, and according to Pliny, never more than thirteen inches wide.

Pliny and Ifidorus have informed us that the Romans had feveral forts of Paper, to which they had given different names. Pliny mentions eight of thefe.

1. *Charta Hieratica,* of which were four different forts.

a. Charta Hieratica. This was a Paper not cleaned at all.

b. Charta

b. Charta Augufta, (fo called to pay refpect to the Emperor Auguftus) was improved by one cleaning.

c. Charta Liviana (named after the Emprefs) which was rendered fuperior by a fecond cleaning.

d. Charta Hieratica. This name was likewife given to Paper in full perfection.

The Romans named thefe four affortments in general *Charta Hieratica,* or Holy Paper, becaufe it was principally ufed for facred books and writings. All were eleven inches wide.

The *Charta Augufta* had at firft the preference, but being too thin for the writingcane, in the fiftieth year after Chrift, under the reign of the Emperor Claudius, it was improved by lining the Auguftan

Paper

Paper with an underlaying of the fame
Paper, which gave the name to

2. *Charta Claudia.* This Paper was
better than *Charta Augufta,* and two inches
wider. I muft obferve, that all books
preferved in *Herculaneum* are written on
Paper not underlaid; and that the firft
Paper was only written on one fide. The
Adverfaria, of which Pliny the elder left
one hundred and fixty volumes, were the
only books preferved in which the leaves
were written on both fides; two leaves
being pafted together. It is faid that
Julius Cæfar was the firft who wrote *opifto-
graphically,* but only when he wrote
letters to confidential friends.

3. *Charta Fannia. Palæmon,* a celebrated grammarian, had in the year five,
feveral public work-fhops, in which this
Paper was prepared with more fkill: it was
ufually ufed for writing plays upon. It
was

was ten inches wide, and glazed with a tooth, ivory, or mufcle-fhells.

4. *Charta Amphitheatrica,* which was much coarfer than the before-mentioned forts, and only nine inches wide.

5. *Charta Saitica,* which was only made in the city of Said, Salo, or Sahid, from the cuttings or fhavings, and refufe of other Paper, which was gathered throughout the country, and re-manufactured in this city: it was not full nine inches wide.

6. *Charta Tanitica,* which obtained that appellation from the city of Tanic, now Damietta.

7. *Charta Emporetica,* or fhopkeeper's Paper, which was ufed to wrap goods in, was manufactured from the next pellicle under the rind of the Papyrus, and fold by weight: but, being only fix inches wide,

it

it was found to be inconvenient for covering
and packing of goods. It has been called
by fome *Leneotica.*

8. *Charta Macrocolla,* or only *Macrocol-
lum.* It received its name from its large
fize.

Several authors mention other forts:
Charta Libyana, which was in quality next
to the *Chartæ Auguſtæ, Charta Thebaica,
Charta Carica, Charta Memphitica, Charta
Corneliana,* after Cornelius Gallus, who was
the firſt that had this paper manufactured.
Mellonis Pagina; Charta Blanca; it obtained
its name from its beautiful whitenefs: this
name is yet applied to a blank ſheet of
Paper, which is only figned. *Charta Nigra*
was the name of Paper painted black, and
the letters written thereupon were of
white and other colours.

The Egyptian Paper was manufactured in
Alexandria

Alexandria and other Egyptian cities, in
fuch large quantities, that Vopifcus fpeaks
of Fermies having boafted, that he poffeffed
fo much Paper, that its value would maintain a large army for a long time. Alexandria was for a confiderable time folely in
poffeffion of this manufacture, and acquired
immenfe riches, which was much noticed
by the Emperor Adrian; and it is not
at all furprizing, that the gain which
the inhabitants of Egypt made from the
trade and confumption of this manufacture, during the fpace of feveral hundred years, was exceedingly great; having
it all to themfelves, and furnifhing Europe and Afia therewith. At the end
of the third century the commerce of
Egyptian Paper was ftill flourifhing, and
continued to the fifth century, notwithftanding it was charged with a very high
impoft, which induced King Theodoric, a
friend to juftice, *after thefe impofts were,*
at the latter end of the fifth century, *greatly
increafed,*

increafed, to deliver Italy therefrom at the commencement of the fixth century. Caffiodorus wrote on that fubject a very remarkable letter (the thirty-eighth letter in his eleventh book) congratulating the whole world on the ceffation of an impoft on an article of commerce, fo neceffary for the convenience and improvement of mankind; and fo highly oppreffive to the cultivation and profperity of arts, fcience, and commerce.

It was ftill ufed occafionally in Italy until the eleventh century, but not generally, by reafon of its laborious, difficult, and expenfive manufacture, and that the ufe of Parchment and Paper made of cotton became gradually introduced. Several authors differ again in ftating the exact period when the ufe of Egyptian Paper was dropt; but this difference may originate from miftaking the Paper made of Papyrus for that of the bark of trees, which was even con-

L   tinued

tinued to be ufed in the twelfth century, and fhall be mentioned hereafter.

Some of that Paper is preferved to the prefent time. It was already known in France in the fifth and fixth centuries. Mabillon quotes feveral acts ftill exifting, written on Paper manufactured from the Papyrus, by the Kings Childebert the Firft and Clodovic the younger; and Gregorius Turonenfis affirms in his letters, that it was generally ufed at an early period in the French Chancery. In the Abbey of St. Germain des Prez, at Paris, was a complete work written on Egyptian Paper. In the Royal Library at Paris was the *Charta plenariæ poteftatis*, written on the fame Paper. And Mabillon remarks that one of fuch manufcripts, written in the fixth century, was in the Library of Mr. Petau, which Montfaucon could not get a fight of.

In the Cottonian Library are four leaves
of

of this Paper, on which the gofpels of St. Matthew and St. John are written.

Italy can produce feveral explanations of Pfalms, manufcripts of the Fathers of the Church, Public Acts, &c. written on Egyptian Paper: amongft them I muft notice a fcarce relick of the treafury of St. Mark, at Venice, which is the gofpel of St. Mark, written by himfelf, of which fome leaves have been conveyed to Prague, by the Emperor Charles IV. It is kept with great veneration and care in a filver cafe gilt, which is in the form of a book, and confidered to be the moft precious piece of the whole treafury, notwithftanding no perfon is able to diftinguifh a fingle letter, being fo much injured by time, that it tumbled to afhes when only touched. Zanetti difcovered in the cabinet of Mr. Nani, a diploma of Papyrus, a Venetian ell long, and half an ell wide. And lately was found, in the archives at Florence, a document

which

which is apparently written between the
years of 454 and 469, of fix feet by two;
many others are exifting in Italy, too numerous to fpecify.

Amongft the feveral documents written
on Egyptian Paper, at Vienna, is a diploma
of Pope Benedict III, of twenty one feet by
two: and a document in Latin, which is
entirely preferved. The record of Ottokar,
King of Bohemia, is likewife written on
Egyptian Paper. In the Electoral Library
at Munich, is a manufcript on reed; and in
the Library at St. Gall in Switzerland, is a
Codex of this Paper, on thirty leaves in
quarto, written in the feventh century,
with *Uncial* letters, containing the *Homi-*
lias St. Auguftini et Ifidori. In the Library
at Geneva are two manufcripts, according
to Mabillon and Montfaucon, of the fourth
and fifth century. I could quote many
more remains of Egyptian Paper, noticed
by Mabillon, Vacchieri, Gerkens, Lambe-
cius,

cius, and other authors; and other manu-
scripts lately discovered by scientific
travellers; but, as it would extend this
account beyond my intended limits, I
shall now turn to another Paper-material,
which is more ancient than the Paper of
Papyrus.

Charta Corticea, or Paper of the Bark of
Trees, manufactured of the *membrana ligni
tenuiori,* and likewise used for writing, is
difficult to be distinguished from the
Egyptian shrub-paper, called *Charta papy-
racea ex pelliculis herbæ Ægyptiacæ;* and
therefore often considered to be the same;
and several authors deny it ever to have
existed. But if they had carefully examined these two sorts, they would have
discovered their error, and the difference.

The *Charta Corticea* has been, as afore-
said, made of the fine skinny substance
separated from the interior side of the bark

L 3

of fuch trees as were fit for that purpofe, which has been moft likely formed into Paper by wafhing, beating, and plaining, like the Paper of Papyrus. But it had always three or four couches, which were glued together, and was therefore through its thicknefs not only more brittle, but the united pellicles often feparated; principally the upper couch which was written on, and the writing became, therefore indiftinct and ufelefs. The *Codices* of *Charta Corticea* are for the major part written in Latin, which gives us reafon to fuppofe, that it was ufed principally in the weftern countries, where the Egyptian Paper could not be obtained, or was very expenfive, and the inhabitants were therefore obliged to try to make their own paper. All ancient documents in Germany which are not written on parchment are in general on Paper made of filk, wool, and the bark of trees; but thefe on Paper made from Papyrus are fcarce, and a much experienced

eye

eye is only able to diftinguifh one from
the other. In the Abbey of St. Germain
is a remnant of a manufcript, the upper
couch of which has difappeared with the
letters. In the archives of the church at
Gironne are preferved the bulls of the
Popes Romànus and Formofus, of the
years 891 and 895. They are about fix
feet long, and three feet wide, and are
apparently formed by gluing the fkins or
leaves couchwife one to the other; and
the writing remains legible in different
places. The learned men in France could
not agree, on the fubftances, of which
this paper had been made, and differed
in their opinions; fome take it to be
Egyptian paper, and others for paper made
of the inner fibres of the bark of trees,
and the laft opinion was fupported by the
majority, which induced the Abbot He-
raut de Belmont to write a treatife on
thofe differences of opinion; and according to the genealogic almanack at Berlin,

of

of the year 1788, many remnants of this curious paper are yet preferved in feveral convents. In the Imperial Library at Vienna is likewife an original preferved, which is a *charte blanche,* granted on this kind of Paper. The ufe of this Paper continued in France till the 12th century.

That, in the moft ancient times, fkins and hides* of animals have been ufed as a writing material I have before stated. In more modern times the fkin between the hide and the flefh was fe-parated, fcraped, and by working and rubbing with quicklime, were formed into leaves, and called *Membrana.* Thefe were ufed by the Hebrews and Greeks; and the

---

Libro in corio, is not the particular name of books written on animal fkins, but many times ufed for books of bark of trees; and, when Ulpianus fpeaks of *libris in corio,* corium fignifies no animal fkin, but the bark of fome other trees than the lime-tree, which has been named *coria.*

the Jews maintain that their anceſtors
uſed them for writing on the Mountain
of Sinai. It is certain that the Jews had
at the time of David, books of the ſkin
of animals rolled up called *Mgilloth*; and
Herodotus aſſures us, that in remote times
the ſkins of ſheep and goats were the
uſual writing materials about 440 years
before Chriſt. That the ancients have
uſed ſkins of different animals for that
purpoſe is apparent, by the words, *Mem-*
brana caprina, agnina, ovilla, vitulina, et
hoedina, which are found in ſeveral authors.

But ſuch membranes are very different
from the true parchment, *Charta Per-*
gamena.

Ptolomæus the Firſt,* King of Egypt,
who died in the year of Rome, 470,
eſtabliſhed in Alexandria, a very extenſive

---

* Sometimes named *Soter* and *Lagus.*

five library, which was much enlarged
by his fon Ptolomæus Philadelphus, with
the affiftance of his librarian Demetrius
Phalereus. Eumenes, King of Pergamus,
as has been before ftated, contended with,
and endeavoured to furpafs him if poffible, which created jealoufy; and caufed
Ptolomæus to prohibit the exportation of
Egyptian Paper, under heavy penalties.
It may be that this prohibition was not
folely occafioned by jealoufy, but from the
fear that his dominions, which were fo
much improved in arts, fciences, and civilization, fince the difcovery of Paper,
would be again reduced to a ftate of
ignorance for want of Paper, becaufe the
plant failed fometimes in unfavourable
weather. The Pergamians were therefore
obliged to devife other means for making
Paper, and they difcovered the manufacture of ufeful parchment, about 300
years before Chrift, and in the fifth century of Rome which obtained its name
from

from the city of Pergam, or Pergamus,
in Afia (now Pergamo), the place where
it was invented, and the art of bringing
it to fuch a ftate of perfection, that according to Prideaux and Freret, it greatly
furpaffed the Egyptian Paper in finenefs,
fmoothnefs, and ftrength; and the art of
making it very thin arrived likewife in a
fhort time to a furprizing degree of perfection. Rome manufactured the beft
parchment. The firft inventor could only
manufacture yellow parchment; yet in
Rome it was foon improved, and made
white: but as that delicate colour was
too liable to tarnifh and fpot, it was only
made white on one fide, and the other
left yellow; and if it was to be ufed for
writing on both fides, it was coloured
violet and purple, and the letters were
written thereon in gold or filver. Gold
was only ufed for facred writings, and
principally for the Pfalms and Gofpels.

Jofephus

Jofephus ftates, that the High-Prieft Eleazar fent to Ptolomaeus Philadelphus a copy of the Holy Scriptures which was to be tranflated into Greek by feventy-two interpreters. The king greatly admired the beauty thereof and the fine membranes, (*tenuitatam membranae*) on which it was written with golden letters. But the tranflation has been made in Egypt only 285 or 286 years before Chrift, by the Synedrion, which confifted, like the Hierofolymitanic, of feventy-two learned men, who not only made the tranflation, before it was laid for the King, and introduced into the fynagogues, but revifed it with fome alterations. It was only the Pentateuch, or the five books of Mofes, becaufe the other parts of the language of the Jews at that time were not confidered as parts of their laws, and therefore lefs neceffary for the Egyptian Jews; and it is clearly proved by the latter part of the book of Efther, that it has been tranflated

tranflated into Greek by another tranf-
lator.

All the world at that time did not
ufe folely Paper and Parchment for writing upon, but ftones and metals; the
laft were chiefly continued on account of
its durability, and all nations had not attained a knowledge of the ufeful inventions of the Egyptians and Pergamians.
Parchment came into ufe in Europe
not before the fixth century, which
increafed in the eighth and ninth; and
England and Germany made very little
ufe of Egyptian Paper for diplomas, but
parchment, till the year 1280. I am informed that before the invention of Rag-
paper, nothing elfe was ufed in Germany
for diplomas than parchment; and, notwithftanding, no map of parchment made
before the fixth century has been difcovered.

With

With refpect to the fize, length, and width of the parchment, it was not regulated like the Egyptian Paper, and there are documents as fmall as our playing-cards. There was likewife no adopted rule, if written at length or at the fides; it depended on every one's fancy: but as it commonly was ufed only on one fide, it was more generally written fidewife than lengthwife, to fave fpace. When printing was invented, parchment was likewife printed upon; and at Berlin, Brunfwic, Paris, and St. Blaife, * are copies of a bible, printed in the year 1450, on parchment, by Guttenburg, in three folio volumes. At the Univerfity library at Helmftadt is the *Officia Ciceronis*: and from the library of the late Mr. von Duve was fold, by public auction, the very fcarce work, printed on parchment, *Chronica Figurata totius mundi a Hartm. Schedelio, Doct.*

---

*An Abbey of the Benedictines, in the Black Foreft, in the Bifhopric of Conftance. The Abbot is a Prince of the German Empire.

Doct. Norimb. of. Anton. Koberger, printed in folio, 1493, with copper-plates.

Parchment fhould be only made of calf-fkins, to be entitled to its name; but it is in modern times likewife made of the fkins of fheep, goats, affes, and hogs. I fhall not enter into a defcription of the manufacture of parchment, or repeat the various ways in which it is ufed, new or old, but only ob-ferve that in France there is annually the value of upwards of a million of livres of parchment manufactured.

Every one well knows that the ufe of parchment is ftill continued in Europe, not only becaufe it is more durable than paper, but alfo that it can be converted into fize when old and ufelefs. But the high price thereof prevents its general ufe; it would be therefore of great confequence to the publick, if a fubftitute could be in-vented, equally as durable as parchment.

Such

Such a difcovery would be highly beneficial, as it would not only encreafe the writing and printing material, but referve fuch a large quantity of animal fkins for the ufe of leather, which becomes daily more fcarce. In many libraries are manufcripts of calves-parchment to be feen with painted pictures. The art of painting on parchment was common before the art of painting with oil-colours was difcovered. The miniature paintings on parchment of Johannes de Brugges, painter to King Charles the Fifth, and thofe of Julio Clavio, which were painted in the year 1500 in the Virgiluis of the Vatican merit to be noticed. And in the palace of the King of Naples has been preferved a book with miniature paintings on parchment, by Macedo, Scholar of Michael Angelo. Parchment takes all kind of colours, but actually is only painted, red, green, and blue; except by the Dutch who dye it likewife yellow, and its principal

beauty

beauty is, that it can be made not only coloured but alfo tranfparent.

I fhall now continue my hiftorical account, and obferve, that it is erroneous to ftate that the Arabs invented, in the eighth century, the manufacture of Paper from cotton: and Cafiri, who ftates it to have been difcovered in the year 706, by Jofeph Amra, cannot deny that it was known before that time by the Chinefe and Perfians. The Arabians are therefore not the inventors, and acquired the knowledge of making it only in 704, by their conquefts in Tartary. This invention became then more generally known, but the art of manufacturing it was only imported in the eleventh century into Europe; and neither is the year of its difcovery precifely known, nor the inventor's name. The firft paper of that kind was made of raw cotton;* but its manufacture

* This muft have been unknown to *Guetard*, or he would not have ftated that he was the firft who had

M   afcertained

manufacture was by the Arabians extended to old worn-out cotton, and even to the fmalleft pieces thereof.

But as there are cotton-plants of various kinds, it is natural that thefe muft have produced papers of different qualities; and it was impoffible to unite their woolly particles fo firmly as to form a ftrong fubftantial Paper, for want of fufficient fkill; and alfo for want of European mills (which are not yet eftablifhed by the Moors, Arabs, and Turks, who make ufe of mortars, and hand

and

---

afcertained by experiment,that raw cotton-wool could be converted into Paper, without being previoufly ufed for clothing or other purpofes. It feems he has been mifled by the Jefuit *du Halde,* who fays that the Chinefe made their Paper from cotton-rags. *Guetard* alfo afferts, that he was induced to make his experiments, becaufe he had not found an author who mentioned the practicability of making Paper from cotton-wool; and that by beating it to a pulp he has made fine white Paper of it. But if he had read *Theophilus Prefbyter* and *Monachus,* he would have been informed that in the Eaftern countries it was cuftomary to make Paper of cotton-wool.

and horfe-mills*), it was impoffible they could bring their wool, by that method, and by boiling and beating, to a fine pulp, rendered intirely free from its woolly quality.

Not

* Thofe who have travelled in Afia and Africa take very little notice of Paper manufactures and mills. Niebuhr declares in the firft volume of his travels (page 150) pofitively, that he faw in Egypt, neither water or wind-mills, and that the publick corn-mill, worked by oxen, at Kahira, was ufed not only for grinding corn, but likewife for preffing oil-cakes; and that the common people grind their corn with very fimple hand-mills. He gives of all thefe mills a defign and defcription, which enables us to afcertain, that they cannot be employed for making paper. The Arabs and Turks give themfelves at prefent very little trouble for making paper, being plentifully fupplied by the Italians and French. There is neverthelefs near Conftantinople, on a rivulet, a paper-mill, which is named in the Turkey language *Kehatjana*, or Paper-manufactory, and makes Cotton-paper. The Greeks ufe water-mills, and built this mill; all the other mills in Conftantinople are Horfe-mills, of which feveral hundred were burnt in Auguft 1782. Du Halde in his travels in 1697 takes no notice of Paper-mills in China, and mentions only a Paper-manufactory at Ming-hya. And Navarette ftates not in his travels, publifhed in folio at Madrid in the year 1676, at *Fon-gan* in his road from To-chew to Pekin, that he faw feveral paper-mills, as is erroneoufly tranflated: he fays only, that he faw feveral paper-manufactures, without naming them paper-mills.

Not difcovering in fuch ancient cotton-
paper, ftripes or water-marks, or the prints
of wire refembling thofe of our moulds, we
muft prefume that their forms were not
like our fkilfully invented moulds, through
which the water runs off, and the mafs
remains therein united.

The Chriftian difciples of Moorifh paper-
makers, who fince 1085, were in poffeffion
of Toledo, and in 1238, of Valencia, worked
the paper-mills to more advantage than their
predeceffors: inftead of manufacturing Paper of cotton-wool (which is eafily recognized by its being brittle and remaining
always yellow), they made it of cotton-
rags, in moulds through which the water
ran off: for this reafon it was called parch-
ment-cloth. Befide thefe denominations,
the hiftorians of that time call it *Charta,*
Xylina, or *Goffypina,* from the cotton-
plant; *Charta Bombycina,* from the fhrub
Bombax, by which name it was likewife
defcribed

defcribed in England; *Charta Cotonea;*
Charta Damafcena; and *Charta Serica.*

All civilized nations ufed firft the Egyptian and then the cotton-paper, but had
not any idea of ufing linen for the fame
purpofe; and to this day the Eaftern nations who manufacture their own Paper,
and even the Greeks, employ only cotton-
wool and cloth for that ufe; and are fo
much accuftomed to ftrongly glazed Paper,
that when they receive Rag-paper from
Italy and the fouth of France, they glaze it
till it refembles our gloffy linen cloth.

It is probable that the Greeks made ufe
of cotton-paper fooner than the Latins.
And that it was brought into Europe by the
Greeks, at an earlier period than by the
Moors from Spain, there is no doubt. The
Greeks received it from the Tartarian coun-
tries at the Bukarias; and through Venice
it came into Germany, where it was known

M 3 in

in the 9th century by the name of Greek
parchment. Greece, fo much connected *
by commerce with Afia and Egypt; Italy,
which was already in the 7th century fre-
quented by the Arabs; Spain, which they
conquered in the 8th century, and poffeffed
to the latter end of the 15th; were, without contradiction, the European countries
where cotton-paper was firft ufed. The
Arabs manufactured, at Cebta (which is,
according to Manjanfius, now Ceuta), a
cotton-paper, called Cebti; and Spain being
fo

---

* The connections of the Greeks with Italy and the
Oriental Empire, and their navigation on the Black-fea,
conveyed the knowledge of cotton-paper eafily to Europe, notwithftanding no document of this paper has
been preferved from Greek antiquity, or noticed before
the time of the Emprefs Irene, wife of the Emperor
Alexius Comnenus, who at the latter part of the eleventh or at the commencement of the twelfth century,
made three copies of the rules for her nuns at Conftantinople, two on parchment, and one on cotton-paper.
The Genoefe and Venetians, who eftablifhed themfelves
afterwards in the Crimea, and carried on commerce
with the Greeks and the countries on the Black-fea,
took care of the exportation of cotton-paper to the Eu-
pean countries.

ſo near, could eaſily have been provided
with it, until manufactories were ſhortly
after eſtabliſhed at Xativa, (or Sateba,)
Valencia, and Toledo.

The ſtuff for this paper, cotton, was moſt
likely cultivated in Spain by the people
who had conquered it, becauſe they came
from a country where it was in general uſe,
and they were therefore accuſtomed to it.
There is yet more than one quality of cotton
cultivated in Spain, and that commodity is
conſidered in the Kingdom of Valencia as a
home production; and it is not unlikely
that the predeceſſors of the Arabs, (the
Phœnicians and Carthaginians,) introduced
it into Spain. Swinburne calculates the
produce of cotton, the growth of Valencia,
at 450,000 arobes, value 350,000l. which
is in ſome meaſure confirmed by Twiſs, who
ſaw, between Cordova and Granada, ſeveral
fields full of cotton-plants* in his travels
through Spain in 1772 and 1773.

The

The paper-manufactories at Xativa, Valencia, and Toledo, produced only very coarfe cotton-paper till the Moors were driven from Spain, either by the Arabians or Chriftians. The Spaniards being acquainted with the ufe of water-mills, improved the method of grinding the cotton-wool and rags; and by ftamping the latter in the mill, they produced a better pulp than from the wool, from which various forts of Paper were manufactured, nearly equal to thofe made of linen-rags.

Spain ftill poffeffes refidues of cotton-paper. At the convent of Silos, is a Latin vocabulary, of intermixed parchment and thick cotton-paper leaves, written in *Gothic* characters, the date of which muft have been prior to the reign of Alphonfus VI. as the

---

*Dillon, in his Travels through Spain, mentions cotton as a natural production, and it is furprifing that *Ulloa*, a Spaniard, in his *Retabliffement des Manufactures et du Commerce de l'Efpagne*, has omitted the mentioning of cotton.

the ufe of *Gothic* writing was forbidden in
1129 at the council at Leon. As very few
manufcripts are found on cotton-paper
from the 10th to the 12th century, but the
major part on parchment, or intermixed, it
muft be fuppofed that at that time cotton-
paper was fcarcer than parchment, or that
this mixture was neceffary becaufe fufficient
parchment could not be obtained, and that
the cotton-paper was too tender and more
liable to break.

The Arabian author, Scherif al Edriffi,
certifies that in 1151 very fine white cotton-
paper was manufaĉtured; and Cacim Aben
Hegi affures us that the beft was made at
Xativa.

The King, Peter II. of Valencia (or the
fourth King of Arragon) iffued, in 1338, a
command to the paper-makers at Valencia
and Xativa, under pain of punifhment, to
manufaĉture better Paper, which was to be
equal

equal to that formerly made. Mr. Meerman had in his poſſeſſion a piece of very coarſe cotton-paper written upon in 1339, which proves that the art of paper-making was neglected by the Spaniards; and that prior to the middle of the 14th century no linen-rag Paper had been manufactured in that country. This has been fully aſcertained by the above gentleman, from the repeated examination of ſeveral pieces of Paper ſent to him for that purpoſe. Notwithſtanding, their ſcientific men perſiſt in its being linen-paper.

Cotton-paper came into uſe in France ſhortly after its invention; and until 1311, no other Paper than this and the Egyptian Paper was known in that country.

At what period cotton-paper was introduced into England cannot be aſcertained with accuracy. The moſt ancient manuſcript which can be produced is of 1049:

and

and it appears that its ufe continued till
the latter end of the 14th century, and
that it has been gradually fupplanted by
the linen-paper, which came into ufe in
1342. All documents written between
1282 and 1347, which Ducarell erroneoufly
ftates to be linen-paper, are written on cotton-paper, as is the *Carmina aurea Salomonis
Regis,* in *His Majefty's library,* compofed
in the fourteenth century, in the Greek
and Latin languages; at leaft there is no
reafon to doubt what Mr. Meerman ftates
on this fubject.

Of the introduction of cotton and linen
Paper into Scotland, nothing can be afcertained; and it is fingular that it has not
been noticed by Thomas Ruddiman. The
fame is the cafe with Ireland. But difcoveries may yet be made in thefe countries.

The knowledge of cotton-paper came by
means of the Greeks to Italy; and the art
of

of making it, in Sicily, through the inva-
fion of the Saracens. It is certain there
was no linen-paper ufed before 1367.

The bulls of the Popes Sergius II. John
XIII. and Agapetus II. were written in
the eighth and ninth centuries, on cotton-
paper. Dufrefne quotes under the article
Charta Cuttunea, from *Rocchi Pyrrhi Sicilia
Sacra*, a place where the family of a paper-
maker is mentioned, but no time is noticed,
notwithftanding a full account is given of a
cotton-paper manufacture which we have
not of any other country.

The large paper-manufacture at Fabriano,
in the *Marchia Anconitana* (which, according to Bartolus's defcription, confifted of
feveral different mills belonging to different
perfons, although the whole formed only
one manufacture), was eftablifhed long ago,
but was enlarged from time to time, and
manufactured, at the period when Bartolus
wrote,

wrote, nothing but cotton-paper. This
author died in 1355; fo that it feems that
1367, or thereabouts, was the time when
linen-paper was brought into ufe in Italy:
and cotton might have been fome time
before mixed with linen-rags, till the fuperiority of the latter was fully afcertained.

As foon as the ufe of cotton-paper was
adopted in Italy, it was alfo introduced
into Germany; and, at the commencement
of the ninth century, well known under
the name of Greek parchment. Germany
imported the paper fome time before it manufactured it; and notwithftanding it received the ftuff through the fame channel
as the Paper, and that cotton and flax were
fpun and wove in the tenth century, the
manufacture of cotton paper cannot be
traced in Germany to fuch an early period:
all that can be pofitively afcertained is, that
in the middle of the fourteenth century, it
was made by ftamping-mills. But as Germany

many had in the thirteenth century, already cotton and linen manufactures, and exported confiderable quantities thereof to Italy, it is fair to prefume that cotton paper was alfo manufactured.

Germany poffeffes numerous well-known relicks of cotton-paper, and amongft the numerous manufcripts preferved in the archives, convents, and libraries, there may be ftill more ancient documents than any which are yet come to our knowledge, and which remain unknown for the want of a precife examination. In the collegiate church and cathedral at Ganderfheim is a *plenarium* of the tenth century, which amongft other rarities of that church boaft of five documents and grants, given by the founders of the convent, between 844 and 968, by the Duke Ludolphus of Saxony, by his fon the Duke Otto, and by the Popes Sergius the Second, Agapetus the Second, and Johannes the Thirteenth. The Plenarium

rium is likewife written on cotton-paper, in
the reign of the Emperor Henry the Second,
and attefted in 1007 with the imperial confirmation by his notary Apel Peranfa. A
large manufcript of 1095 is at the Imperial
Library at Vienna. The Univerfity Library
at Erlangen has a collection of 420 manufcripts on parchment, and 150 on cotton-
paper. In the convent at Weirgarten are
preferved numerous codices and manufcripts of all centuries, and on every kind of
materials and paper. In the convent at
Rheinau are 490 manufcripts on different
kinds of paper. The library at the Vatican
contained 50,000 volumes, amongft which
there were 17,000 manufcripts. In the city
library at Augfburgh are numerous manufcripts, and many of them in Greek
more valuable than thofe at the Vatican.
The Library of the Convent at Tegernfee
contains 1500 manufcripts of the 8th, 9th,
10th, 11th, 12th, 13th, 14th, and 15th
centuries; and in the Abby of St. Blaife, are
fome

fome of the fifth century. The univerfity Library at Harlem, and the Library of the Abby St. Emeran are rich in old manufcripts; and the chapter at Salzburgh produces 58 *Codices chartaceos,* of cotton Paper, amongft its collections.

I now conclude the hiftorical account of the feveral fubftances which have been ufed as writing materials, with the invention of linen Paper.

The Royal Society of Sciences, at Gottingen, has, in the years 1755 and 1763, offered premiums to trace the exact time of this difcovery; and Mr. Meerman printed in 1762 at Rotterdam, *Gerardi Meerman, Syndici Roterodamenfis, Admonitio de Chartæ noftratis, feu lineæ, origine,* and offered 25 ducats to find it out. All refearches were loft and reduced to an uncertainty, through the exifting remnants of cotton Paper, which was as before ftated in ufe fome centuries before

before the linen Paper, becaufe thefe two
are in many refpects fimilar, and cotton
and linen rags may have been at firft mixed,
which rendered it therefore more difficult
to afcertain when the firft Paper was made
from linen rags alone.

The Jefuit Du Halde attributes this invention to the Chinefe; but as Gerbillon,
and other modern travellers affure us that
in the Paper-manufacture at Ming-hya, raw
hemp was beaten and macerated with drugs,
and then manufactured into Paper, this
nation cannot exclufively claim the difcovery of the art of making Paper from
linen rags; and all authors agree that Europe
is entitled to the merit of this invention, but
they differ as to the time;* fome trace it to
the

* Hertius, who feemingly had no knowledge of cotton-
paper, believes linen-paper was invented in the fixth
century.

Orlandi quotes a manufcript of Homer in the
Library at Geneva, written on linen-paper before the
year 8co.

N   Muratori

the 8th, 10th, and others to the 11th and 12th century; and it is moſt likely that Paper has been made from linen cloth before it was attempted to be made from linen rags.

It is to be obſerved, that the invention of making paper from linen, has been preceded by the art of making paper of cotton-rags, which muſt be conſidered as a preparatory ſtep towards the uſe of linen-rags for the ſame purpoſe. But as this required ſome time, and improvements of the firſt diſcovery, it is therefore more natural that this invention

---

Muratori believes that linen-paper has been firſt named *Charta bombycina*, and invented in the tenth or eleventh century.

Harduin will make us believe, that he has ſeen acts and diplomas written on linen-paper before the twelfth century; and Caſiri ſays; *Non pauca in regia Eſcurialenſi Bibliotheca extant monumenta, quae ante tertium decimum Chriſti ſeculum ſunt exarata.*

But Montfaucon ſtates the contrary, and inſiſts that he has not diſcovered, either in France or Italy, a book, inſtrument, or manuſcript written on linen-paper previous to *Ludovicus ſanctus*, who died ſince 1270.

vention is to be afcribed, to a country, which was more familiar with linen, and its agriculture, than with the application of cotton.

Gregorius Majanfius, of Oliva; Francifcus Perez, of Toledo; and Ferdinando Velafco, of Madrid, endeavoured to trace this difcovery in Spain, but could not prove that their country was entitled to the merit of it, being completely defeated by a number of other authors; and it feems that the Spaniards had no knowledge of linen Paper before the middle of the fourteenth century, and then it was not manufactured in that country, but imported; and it is moft likely linen and linen-rag Paper were only manufactured in Spain a fhort time before the art of printing was introduced. Spain cannot therefore claim the merit of this invention; notwithftanding feveral places in Spain produce very good flax;* and even

foon

* Twifs relates that he found in the kingdom of Valencia

foon after that they manufactured Paper
from linen rags, thefe manufactories went
to

---

lencia flax and hemp in abundance, where the commoneſt
clafs of the people wore linen apparel. He obferves
alfo that the fruitful plains of Granada produced likewife flax and hemp. The cultivation of hemp and flax
is at prefent very confiderable; in Valencia are annually 25,000 cwt. of hemp, and 30,000 cwt. of flax
cultivated. The exportation of hemp from Aragonia
was in 1775, 22,000 cwt. But it is certain, that Spain
confumes at leaſt ten times more flax and hemp than it
cultivates, and even this was then not manufactured,
being in the habit of purchafing their linen, fails, and
cordage from France, England, Germany and the
Northern Countries. According to Pluce, there has
been imported in the year 1765 in Sevilla, foreign
linen-cloth to the amount of 1,200,000 dollars (270,000*l.*)
In the kingdom of Spain has been imported 24,000 cwt
of flax. Since the foundation and eſtabliſhment of the
Patriotic Society in Spain, the linen-manufacture is
more flouriſhing, and the hemp and flax of their own
growth is not only manufactured, but alfo large quantities of imported. In Barcelona has been manufactured,
in 1783, linen cloth to the value of thirty millions of
reals. But as long as hemp, imported from Riga, with
the duty paid thereon, can be fold at a lower price in
Spain, than its own growth, the cultivation will not be
cheriſhed, and equal the actual profperity of the linen
manufactories; and notwithſtanding the flax and hemp
plant is difperfed all over Europe, its cultivation is ſtill
more proper for the Northern climate.

to decay, becaufe the Kings of Spain firft granted monopolizing privileges to many convents for the manufacture of Paper; and when it came again into private hands, they fixed fuch a low price on printed books, of which the Genoefe availed themfelves, and procured confiderable quantities of rags from Spain, principally from Andalufia; and in 1720, they fent Paper back to Spain to the amount of 500,000 piaftres. There are at prefent upwards of 200 Papermills in Spain, 31 of which are at Alcoi, and Francifco Guarro manufactures Paper as good as any Dutch.

Peris communicated to Majanfius fome works of Ariftotle, tranflated in the year of the world 5010, from the Arabic, by Mofes Semuel Bar Ichdua Ben Thibun at Granada, which is in the year of Chrift 1250. The two different forts of paper, on which was written in Hebrew, out the Royal Library at the Efcurial, and fent by

N 3   Majanfius

Majanſius to Meerman, have on examination been found to be white linen-paper;
they were written at the end of the reign
of Alphonſus the Tenth, and at the commencement of the reign of his ſon Sanctius,
between the years 1280 and 1290. But
notwithſtanding it is decided by thoſe Antiquarians, to be linen-paper, it differs ſo
much in quality and colour from all other
paper manufactured in Spain, that it is more
probable that it has been copied in later
years on imported paper, and the date written thereupon, is by no means a poſitive
proof of its antiquity. The moſt ancient
linen-paper which can be with certainty
traced is of 1367; it is a piece of a manuſcript of *Franciſci Eximii Vita & actis
Chriſti,* and is intermixed with ſheets of
parchment. It has ſcizzars for a watermark,
which was one of the uſual watermarks in
Germany and Italy in the fifteenth century.

France made an early uſe of linen Paper,
but

but manufactures were later eftablifhed
there than in Spain and Italy. Lint or flax,
was cultivated by the Gauls at an early
period; but the clothing with linen became
only a cuftom many centuries afterwards;
and the authors of the eighth century quote
as a remarkable thing that the holy Segolena
was dreffed in a linen fhift, and that the
Queen of France, wife of Charles the Se-
venth, was the firft French Queen who wore
fhifts of linen cloth; which was in the fifteenth century. This is not a proof that no
Paper was made of linen before that time.
Several authors prove the ufe of linen Paper
in 1270, 1294, 1302, 1314, and 1316, but
not that it has been manufactured in France,
and we have no account for feveral centuries
what kind of linen Paper was made in that
country, which the authors would not have
left unnoticed; and therefore no Paper manufacture can be traced before the fifteenth
century. Thefe manufactures became in a
fhort time very flourifhing, and the French

foon

foon exceeded their neighbours in the art of making Paper, and were therefore enabled to export confiderable quantities, which encreafed fo much yearly, that in 1658, of thirty-five millions of livres exported in goods and merchandize to Holland, two millions in value were of Paper ; and it provided Spain, England, Switzerland, Denmark, Sweden, Ruffia, but chiefly Holland and the Levant, with Paper for printing and writing. The Paper manufactures in Languedoc, Lionefe, Guienne, Bretagne, and Poitou work principally for exportation; and the fourteen mills in Alface, which manufacture about 40,000 reams of Paper annually, export about two-thirds thereof to Switzerland and Germany.

As the French ftill export a confiderable quantity of Paper, I think it worthy of notice, to ftate the names, length, width, and weight of all the different forts of Paper, now manufactured in France.

Names.	Length		Width.		A Ream ſhould weigh	And at leaſt
	in.	lin.	in.	lin.		
Grand Aigle . . .	24	9	36	6	131 lb. and upwards	126lb.
Grand Soleil .	24	10	36	0	112 lb. not excᵍ 120 lb.	105
Au Soleil	20	4	29	6	86 and upwards	80
Grand Fleur de Lis .	22	0	31	0	70 not exceeding 74	66
GrandColombier ou } Imperial . . }	21	3	31	9	88 and upwards	84
A l'Elephant . . .	24	0	30	0	85 ditto	80
Chapelet	21	6	30	0	66 ditto	60
Petit Chapelet . .	20	3	29	0	60 ditto	55
Grand Atlas . . .	24	6	26	6	70 ditto	65
Petit Atlas	22	9	26	4	65 ditto	60
Grand Jeſus ou Su-} per Royal . }	19	6	26	0	53 ditto	48
Grand Royal etranger	18	0	25	0	50 ditto	47
Petite Fleur de Lis .	19	0	24	0	36 ditto	33
Grand Lombard .	20	0	24	6	36 not exceeding 40	32
Grand Royal . .	17	10	22	8	32 and upwards	29
Royal . . .	16	0	22	0	30 ditto	28
Petit Royal . . .	16	0	20	0	22 ditto	20
Grand Raiſin . . .	17	0	22	8	29 ditto	25
Lombard . . .	18	0	21	4	24 ditto	22
Lombard ordinaire .	16	6	20	6	22 ditto	20
Cavalier . . .	16	2	19	6	16 ditto	15
Petit Cavalier . .	15	2	17	6	15 ditto	14
Double Cloche .	14	6	21	6	18 ditto	16
Grand Licorne à la } Cloche . }	12	0	19	6	12 ditto	11
à la Cloche . .	10	9	14	6	9 ditto	8
Carré, ou Grand} Compte, ou Sabre, } Sabre au lion . }	15	6	20	0	18 ditto	16
Carré très mince . .	15	6	20	0	13 ditto	13
A l'écu, ou moyen} Compte, Compte } ou Pomponne . }	14	0	19	0	20 ditto	15
à l'écu très mince .	14	2	19	0	11 ditto	11
Au Coutelas . . .	14	2	19	0	17 ditto	16

Names.	Length		Width		A Ream should weigh	And at least
	in.	lin.				
Grand Meſſel . . .	15	0	19	0	15 and upwards	14
Second Meſſel . . .	14	0	17	6	12 ditto	11
à l'étoile, à l'éperon, ou longuet .	13	10	18	6	14 ditto	13
Grand Cornet .	13	6	17	9	12 not exceeding 14	10
Grand Cornet très mince . . .	13	6	17	9	8 and leſs	—
Champy, ou Baſtard	13	2	16	11	12 and upwards	11
à la Main	13	6	20	3	13 ditto	12
Couronne, ou Griffon	13	0	17	1	12 ditto	10
Couronne, ou Griffon très mince	13	0	17	1	7 and leſs	—
Telliere grand Format	13	2	17	4	12 and upwards	10
Cadran	12	8	15	3	11 ditto	10
La Telliere .	12	8	16	0	12½ ditto	11½
Pantalon	12	6	16	0	11 ditto	10
Petit Raiſin, ou Bâton Royal, ou Petit Cornet à la grande ſorte	12	0	16	0	9 or leſs	8
Les trois O ou trois ronds, ou Genes	11	6	16	0	9 and upwards	8½
Petit nom de Jeſus .	11	0	15	1	7½ ditto	7
Aux armes d'Amſterdam Pro Patria ou Libertas .	12	1	15	6	12 to 13	12
Cartier grand Format, Dauphine	13	6	16	0	14 and upwards	12
Cartier grand Format	12	6	16	0	13 ditto	12
Cartier . . .	11	6	15	1	11 ditto	10
Au Pot, ou Cartier ordinaire . .	11	6	14	6	10 ditto	9
Pigeon, ou Romaine .	10	4	15	2	10 ditto	8½
Eſpagnol . .	11	6	14	6	9 ditto	8
Le Lis	11	6	14	1	9 ditto	8
Petit à la Main, ou Main Fleurie .	10	8	13	8	8 ditto	7½
Petit Jeſus . . .	9	6	13	3	6 ditto	5½

All forts which are lefs than nine inches
and fix lines in length, are permitted to be
made of fuch a width as may be required.

That Paper called *Trace, Treſſe, Etreſſe,*
or *Main-brune,* and of the names *Brouillard,*
and *à la Demoiſelle,* and all coloured Papers
may be manufactured of fuch length, width,
and weight as ordered.

There are three forts of French Paper
which are exported to the Levant, that are
not above defcribed:

	Inches.	Inches.	
Aux trois Croiffans, Façon de Venife,	12½ 0 long,	17 0 wide,	20lb. 0oz.
Aux trois Croiffans, ou trois lunes,	12 0	16 0	14 10
Croifette	11 6 lines,	15 5 lines	9 4

The Papers called *Couronne, Cartier,* and
à la Cloche, if defigned for the Levant trade,
differ from the before-mentioned fize and
weight. In *Savary's Dictionnaire Univerfel
de Commerce* are mentioned twenty different
forts

forts of common Paper, made out of old nets and cords, maculated and blotting Paper, to which the French have likewife given different names, but I have omitted them, as they do not contribute to the knowledge of the commerce with Paper, nor to improve and extend our manufactures, which was the motive I had for giving here fo long a detail; whereas I have endeavoured to abbreviate this hiftorical account, in other refpects, as much as poffible. I will now continue to defcribe the remaining forts of Paper manufactured in France.

Demoifelle mince is made of the fineft threads of fifhing nets, and being more ftamped in the mill, lofes its natural colour, and becomes of a cinnamon colour.

Demoifelle forte is lefs ftamped, and of a dark brown colour.

Jofeph

Joſeph Raiſin, and *Quarré Muſe,* are
made of. coarſer nets and cords, which are
not ſtamped fine. Theſe two ſorts are uſed
for packing up the linen cloth at St. Quen-
tin, Beauvois, and Troyes, becauſe their
dark brown colour ſets off the whiteneſs of
the cloth; and it ſeems that the manufacturers put ſome lamp-black in the engine,
to darken the colour.

The Paper, called *Papier à Sacs,* is made
of the coarſeſt rags, and is ſold by weight;
it is ſurpriſingly brittle, and the manufacturers are therefore ſuſpected of mixing it
with ſomething to encreaſe the weight, or
it could not be ſo tender.

At the latter end of the laſt century the
art of making Paper arrived to a great degree of perfection in England and Holland,
ſo that the ſale in France has not ſince been
ſo extenſive, and many Paper-mills have
been ſhut up, or converted to other
purpoſes.

purpofes. There were, a century ago, in the provinces of Perigord and Angoumois 400 Paper-mills, and now there are not one hundred remaining. But the exportation of Paper from France remains neverthelefs very confiderable; and it ftill manufactures, after England and Germany, the largeft quantity of Paper of any country in Europe. It exports very large quantities of all forts, chiefly that manufactured for Paper-hang-ings, to the United Provinces of America, for which reafon, on the 29th of Decem-ber 1787, the exportation-duty on paper fhipped for that country was not only taken off, but alfo the excife returned. At Montargis is the largeft paper-mill, erected to work with 30 vats, which would confume 1,620,000lb. of rags, and 135,000lb. of fize, but want of water, and the quality thereof, has prevented its working to its full extent At Vougeot, in Burgundy, is another large mill, with 12 engines and 20 vats, erected by Mr. Defventes, of which Mr. De La-

lande

lande has furnifhed the public with a complete defcription, and the drawings of all
its parts and machineries.

The printing and writing-papers manufactured in Auvergne are preferred to all other
French paper, except that manufactured
by Mathieu Johannot d'Annonay, which is
principally efteemed for printing copper-
plates. At Thiers are fifteen paper-mills,
which bring beautiful writing-paper to the
market; and at Ambert, where there are
50 paper-mills, and in Angoumois, principally printing-paper is manufactured, of a
very good quality, the moft part of which
is fold at Bourdeaux, and exported to Holland : it is not fized, but much ftronger
preffed. In Limoges are 51 paper-mills,
which work 66 vats. In Normandy, and
the environs of Rouen and Caen, are numerous paper-mills. The valleys near Rouen
provides Paris principally with copy and
packing-paper. In the fmall compafs of
three

three leagues, near Rouen, are 34 paper-
mills; and in a circle of 15 leagues, are
20 others. There were formerly many
more, fome of which were converted in
1748 to other purpofes, principally fulling-
mills. In the Franche-comté are 27 paper-
mills, which work with 30 vats, and are
fituated on the foot of rocks, where they
have a conftant fupply of clear water;
they export their Paper principally to
Switzerland.

The paper-manufacture attained to perfection in France much fooner than in Holland
and England; which, with the cheapnefs
of labour, gave them a certain fuperiority
in foreign markets, which has gradually di-
minifhed, and will remain fo, if no new
improvements and inventions contribute to
its rife. Mr. Robert Lewis in France two
years ago difcovered a way to make, with
one man, and without fire, by means of
machines, fheets of Paper of a very large
fize,

fize, even 12 feet wide, and 50 feet long
He has obtained a patent *.

In France are ftill upwards of 500 Paper-
mills, which confume annually 20,000,000
weight

* This improvement in the art of making Paper will
occafion a revolution in that manufacture, and if brought
to perfection, enable them to underfell in foreign markets, becaufe three men are now required for every
fheet of paper: if now one man is able to make as expe-
ditioufly fheets of fuch a large fize, where upwards of 300
fheets may be cut out, it is of a very great advantage to
the manufacturer, who will thereby be enabled to make
900 fheets of paper with the fame expence of labour, as
he is now obliged to pay for a fingle fheet; and moreover
he will be able to furnifh perfect larger fheets of paper,
than any other heretofore made, and which is much
wifhed for, for drawing and feveral other purpofes.
Mr. Gamble, who arrived in London about twelve
months ago, brought over feveral fheets from France,
and has obtained a Patent which will in fome refpects
contribute to the introduction of this improvement in
the art of making paper in this country; others have
likewife for months paft employed agents in France, to
purchafe fuch machineries for ufe in this country, and
if brought to a greater perfection, there is no doubt, it
will be generally adopted and ufed in the Britifh Paper-
mills, and that their commerce will not be injured by
this difcovery in France.

O

weight of rags and coarfe paper ftuff. In Franche-Comté it was afcertained by the exchequer, that 16,000 cwt. of rags were collected within one year, of which 8,000 were manufactured in that county, and 8,000 exported to other counties: as Franche-Comté is only about one twentieth part of France, 320,000 cwt. of rags muft be annually collected in that country, and upwards of one-third, or 14,000,000 weight are ftill exported, notwithftanding the fevere prohibition.

In Switzerland, efpecially in the principality of Neufchatel (which belongs to the King of Pruffia) and in the Cantons of Bern and Bafil feveral Paper-mills are now eftablifhed, which manufacture very good Paper, admired for its ftrength and whitenefs, which diminifhes the importation from France, and the manufactures at Pontartier. The paper-mill of Mr. Blume, in the canton of Bafil, has gained a fuperiority

in

in that country, and produces copper-plate
paper equal to any manufactured in France.

The time when linen Paper came into
ufe in Italy remains likewife uncertain;
and as all that has come to the knowledge
of the prefent time, cannot be fatisfactorily
afcertained, I will therefore quote only
what may be regarded as authentic. The
fenate of Venice granted, the 19th of Auguft
1366, an exclufive privilege to the Paper-
mill at Trevifo, that no linen Paper-fhavings
or offal fhould be exported from Venice
than for the ufe of that mill; if now fhavings from linen Paper exifted, it proves
the manufacture of that Paper muft have
been eftablifhed fome time before; a document of a notary, in 1367, proves likewife
the ufe of linen Paper; Maffei ftates, that
he is in poffeffion of a family manufcript of
linen Paper, written in 1367, and he attempts therefore to appropriate the invention of linen Paper to Italy, notwithftanding

it

it appears more likely, that by the manufactures of cotton paper, the linen paper
has not been manufactured in Italy at such
an early period. In 1374 the patent of the
manufacture at Trevifo, which proved fuccefsful, was renewed by the fenate of Venice. An extenfive commerce in Paper
was carried on at Venice for exportation.
The city of Gorlitz received, from 1376
to 1426, all its Paper from that country.

Angelus Roccha mentions a Paper manufacture at Foligni, exifting in the 16th century; and he fays, that at Fabriano was manufactured the beft large Paper; and at Foligni, the beft Paper of a fmall fize. The
Paper-mills at Fabriano are yet in efteem, and
there are the greateft number in Italy. In
the Pope's territory at Tivoli, Viterbo, Ron-
ciglione, Bracciano, and Rome, are many
Paper-mills, but they do not make fo much
Paper as they might, from the quantity of
rags gathered in that country; and Schlozer
ftates,

ftates, that one million in weight is annually exported to Genoa. The value is entered at 100,000 fcudi, or crowns.

Venice exports large quantities of Paper to the Levant,* and inferior affortments to the Auftrian dominions: at Colli, in Tufcany,

* The commerce of Paper to Turkey is principally carried on at Venice: the affortments are white, thick, and very clofe: the Turks cannot make ufe of any weaker Paper, becaufe they ufe a reed for writing, which is cut into the form of a pen. Thofe called *fioretto* and the *three moons* are in the greateft requeft, being very ftrong and very heavy. The *fioretto* is the moft fafhionable kind of Paper, and the deareft. The Turks gum it, and brighten it with a polifhing-inftrument.

Next to Venice, Genoa is the place in Italy which exports the greateft quantity of Paper to the Levant. The Genoefe Papers are much lighter and not fo dear as thofe of Venice: they are made ufe of in winter in-ftead of window-glafs, for œconomy.

Upon the whole, Italy fends Paper into Greece to the amount of 25,000*l.* and into Turkey to the amount of 250,000*l. which ought to be noticed by our mer-chants and Paper-manufacturers*, and engage them in a competition with the Italians in this important branch of the Levant trade, principally as Marfeille has been, of late years, the only place in France that can circulate any of its Papers in Turkey.

Tufcany, is a mill which manufactures very good Paper. In the environs of Turin are feveral mills which furnifh fine Paper; one Paper-maker in Venice is in poffeffion of the fecret of covering his Paper with a varnifh, by which means the writings can be eafily obliterated with a fponge, and he has found an extenfive fale for this Paper. The Genoefe had fome time ago monopolized the Paper-trade of Italy, by manufacturing it of a fuperior quality and whitenefs, and by ufing a particular fize, which it is faid prevented its deftruction by moths; but this commerce is now greatly reduced.

Germany difputes with Italy the moft ancient knowledge of cotton and linen Paper. There were already in the 13th century cotton and linen manufactories eftablifhed, which exported large quantities of goods to Italy and to the Levant; and it cannot therefore be furprifing that the art of inventing linen-rag Paper

is

is judged to belong to Germany: but nothing has been afcertained with certainty. The feveral ancient manufcripts and pieces of linen Paper preferved in Germany do not pofitively afcertain that the firft manufacture was eftablifhed in that country. There have been always quoted two diplomas, to prove the age of the ufe of linen Paper in Germany.; the one is of Count Adolphus the Fourth, of Schaumburgh, who therein confers in 1239 on Rinteln the right and privileges of a city, and which has been made known to antiquarians by Profeffor von Peftel at Leiden; the other is of the year 1303, which Profeffor Popowitfch at Vienna declares to have feen in the archives of the city of Windifchgraetz in 1740. Both diplomas would be mifleading others, if accepted as proofs of the antiquity of linen Paper in Germany; that at Windifchgraetz is only quoted by memory, and the other of Rinteln is ftill more

fufpicious,

fufpicious, and wants the day and month when executed, which is found in all other diplomas given by the faid Count Adolphus, and according to Spangenberg and Bierling, Rinteln did not receive the right and privileges of a city till the year 1340, which is 101 years later. But one piece of Paper, of 1308, which Mr. von Senkenberg fent, in 1763, to Mr. Meerman, merits particular attention; it was ftrong, white, pliable, and had the marks of the wire-moulds, which are the tokens of linen Paper; it was neverthelefs glazed, and much refembled parchment, which are tokens of cotton Paper. The Royal Society of Sciences at Gottingen judged therefore, if the date could be taken as certain, that the epocha could alfo be taken for the true time when linen Paper was invented, notwithftanding Profeffor Murray believes it to be mixed Paper, of linen and cotton, manufactured at Fabriano. If it fhould be linen Paper

manu-

manufactured in Germany, it muſt have
been, according to their opinion, on the
frontiers of Italy.

Von Stetten is of opinion that linen
Paper was manufactured at Augſburgh earlier than in any other part of Germany.
That city was the firſt which eſtabliſhed
conſiderable linen-manufactories, and carried
on in ancient times an extenſive commerce
in linen. Neverthelefs, the eſtabliſhment
of mills cannot be aſcertained, nor the preciſe time when the firſt paper-mill was
built on the Sinkel-ſtream. Longolius at
Hoff endeavours to eſtabliſh it as a fact, that
linen Paper has been made at Augſburgh at
the commencement of the fourteenth century, by a diploma in the archives of the
Prince of Onolzback, by the Biſhop Frederick of Augſburgh, which is without date,
and it ſtates that the ſaid biſhop was of the
houſe of Speet von Thurnegg, who reigned
between the years 1307 and 1330, that the

Paper

Paper muſt therefore have been manufactured within or before that period. This diploma is, on the ſtricteſt examination, declared
to be Paper made from linen; but Meerman ſtill retains his doubts, becauſe another
Biſhop of the name of Frederick reigned in
Augſburgh in 1414, and that there are
yet exiſting in Augſburgh publick accounts
up to the year 1330 all on cotton Paper,
in which repeatedly expenſes are brought
in *pro papyro*, without mentioning if for
linen or cotton Paper.

That Pomerania had an early knowledge
of Paper, has been ſatisfactorily proved by
John Samuel Heringen, Profeſſor at Stettin.
He quotes a long liſt of ſignatures of the
notaries to certify numerous diplomas from
the Dukes of Pomerania, between the years
1263 and 1373. But we cannot take him
for a ſufficient judge of linen and cotton
Paper, and therefore not deciſive in opinion.
A copy of a document of 1289, written in

1315 in monkiſh charaĉters, containing a
donation from Biſhop Hermanzus to the
convent of nuns at Coſlin, has the water-
mark of a bull's head with a croſs on the
top of a pike, raiſed between the horns;
and Heringen believes, that this water-
mark is an undeniable proof, that this Paper
was made in Pomerania, in the diocefe of
the Biſhop of Camin, and that the ſign of
the bull's head muſt be the arms of the
family von Wachold, and that the croſs is
the ſign of the biſhop. But this opinion
muſt be erroneous, even if we admit the
water-mark to be a proof in what country
the Paper has been made. The bull's head
is the arms of Mecklenburgh, and the
German princes are jealous of permitting
their arms to be uſed by any branch of
the nobility, not belonging to their own
houſe. The water-mark, in the firſt invention of linen-paper, may have ſignified in
what parts the Paper has been made, but
has been ſince uſed to diſtinguiſh the quality

 of

of the Paper, or in which mill it was manufactured.

The water-mark of a bull's head in the Paper, which is not in any Italian Paper, and which fcientific men take as an undeniable token of books printed in the firft printing-office of Fauft, is only the firft water-mark made in the moft ancient German linen Paper, and is found in all ancient German manufcripts, and the firft printed books, with fome alterations and additions: the firft manufactured Paper of Germany is of the year 1312, with the water-mark of a plain bull's head, which may have been fince adopted by Paper-makers of other countries, as it is ftill in practice with many forts of Paper that are in great demand; for example, the words *Pro Patria*, which are water-marks in Paper like our foolfcap, originated in Holland, but it is likewife made ufe of in French and German mills; and if the fign of a bull's or bullock's head,

which

which are truly the arms of Mecklenburgh, is to be taken as a proof that the firſt Paper was made in that country which uſes theſe arms, then is Mecklenburgh entitled to the honour of this diſcovery. This is ſupported by the ſituation of Mecklenburgh being on the frontiers of Pomerania.

In the archives at Wolgaſt is a document on linen Paper of 1393. In that of the hoſpital at Kaufbeuren are two of 1318, and in the archives of the city ſeveral others of 1324, 1326, and 1333. Von Murr found in Nuremberg linen Paper of 1319. The moſt ancient linen Paper preſerved in the Netherlands, is the copy of a Bible in verſe, by Jacob Maerlant, in the library of Iſaac le Long, which Meerman ſaw and examined, when the library was ſold by publick auƈtion at Amſterdam, in 1744. A manuſcript in Dutch, " *Het boek der Byen*" of 1330 written on linen Paper, is in the library of Hulſian. At Hohenloe is a
document

document written in 1333, on the Friday
after the Afcenfion. In the convent at
Quedlinburgh is a bill of feoffment, granted
by the Emperor Charles the Fourth, to the
Abbefs Ermingarde in 1339. Bohuflaus Bal-
binus afferts that in the archives at Prague
are preferved feveral diplomas written before
1340, which have induced many to believe
that the firft linen Paper was made in Bohemia. In the library of the Minfter at Fulda,
are preferved with the manufcripts and
letters of celebrated men, fome *Decreta
Judicialia* of the ancient abbots from 1341
to 1491, all written on linen Paper and
with feals. John Daniel Fladd in Heidelf-
berg difcovered feveral documents written
on linen Paper in the fourteenth century,
the moft ancient of which was in 1342. The
Royal Society of Sciences at Gottingen ad-
judged to him a prize-medal of 25 ducats,
for the difcovery of the moft ancient linen
Paper. Helmftadt has exhibited a document of 1343; it is a little deed of an

acre

acre of land, which a prieft of Helmftadt purchafed, and on which are two feals; and as he was in fear for the lafting of his document, the Paper being fo thin, he applied to the magiftrate for a duplicate on parchment, which is only two years younger. In the archives at Plaffenburgh is a record with a feal, dated 1347; and at Magdeburgh are feveral of 1350. Qualenbrinck at Utrecht difcovered, in the bailiwick of Utrecht, three documents of the Teutonic order, two of 1353, and one of 1369. Fladd difcovered another document on linen Paper of 1377, on the back of which is a wax feal; the Paper is rough, and the watermarks very plain. Gatterer at Gottingen found in the family archives of Holzfchuher at Nuremberg a linen Paper document, with the feal on wax of Frederic Holzfchuher, Knight of the Teutonic Order. The library of Paulin at Leipzig poffeffes a manufcript of the poet Hugo Trimberg, written in 1391.

It

It feems, by the numerous relics of an-cient linen Paper in Germany, that it came into ufe there at the beginning of the 14th century, and Ulman Stromer of Nurem-berg, who died in 1407, began in 1360 to write the firft work ever publifhed on the art of Paper-making, and eftablifhed a large Paper-mill in 1390. He employed a great number of perfons, amongft whom were three Italians, Francifcus, Marcus de Marchia, and Bartholomæus; all of them were obliged to make oath not to teach any perfon the art of Paper-making, or to make Paper for their own account. He employed another perfon of the name of George Thirman, who bound himfelf only for ten years. In the firft year he employed two rollers, which fet eighteen ftampers in motion; but when he would in the fecond year add another roller, he was oppofed by the Italians whom he employed, who would not confent to the enlarging of his manu-facture; but they were imprifoned by the

magiftrates,

magiftrates, and then they fubmitted by renewing their oaths.

All the Paper-mills erected, fince the art of printing has been invented by Kofter, of Haaerlem, in 1430, cannot be brought forward as a teftimony to prove the invention of linen Paper-making in Germany; but, after the noble invention of printing (by which ideas can be fo eafily conveyed and difperfed) came in practice, the rapid extenfion and the multiplication of printing made the increafe of Paper-mills neceffary. In the environs of the Rhine, in Swabia, Franconia, Alfatia, Mifnia, and Bohemia, are the greateft number of Paper-mills. In the Hanoverian dominions are 34, and Beyer ftates that there are in Germany 500 Paper-mills* (thofe in Auftria and Pruffia not included), which manufacture at leaft 2,500,000

---

* I fubjoin here an account of fome Paper-mills in Germany, as far as I could obtain knowledge thereof.

1. In

2,500,000 reams of Paper. According to
Count

---

1. In the Circle of Upper Saxony, in the Chur-Mark . 4
   Chur-Saxony 80
   Swedifh-Pomerania 2
2. In the Circle of Lower Saxony, in the Hanoverian
   Dominions 34
   Mecklenburgh 6
   Near Hamburgh 2
3. In the Circle of Weftphalia, in the Principality of
   Minden 1
   County of Lippe 6
   Abbey of Werden 3
   County of Tecklenburg and Linden 3
   In the Circle of the Upper Rhine, in the County of
   Ifenburg 2
   Catzenellenbogen 2
   Hanau-Münzenberg 1
5. In the Circle of Franconia, in the County of Henneberg 3
6. In the Circle of Suabia, near Augfburg 4
   Ulm 1
7. In the Circle of Bavaria, near Regenfburg 1
8. In Bohemia 81
9. In Silefia, in the Environs of Hirfchberg 4
   Sagan 2
   Wartenberg 2
   Schweidnitz 12

Which amount to 256

It is therefore apparent that there muft be more than
500 Paper-mills in Germany.

Large

Count Ewald von Hertzberg, there were, in
1785, in the Pruffian dominions 800 Paper-
manufactures, the revenue thereof produced
200,000 dollars annually.

Large fums of money go notwithftanding
from Germany to foreign countries, for the
purchafe of Paper, becaufe the Paper-
makers make in general coarfe Paper chiefly
for printing, and the finer forts and writing-
paper are imported. In the port of Hamburgh were imported, in 1782, 7,439 bales
(of 10 reams and upwards,) 4,336 reams;
four cafks, and three chefts, with Paper.
That city has no more than two Paper-mills,
of two vats each, which confume 6,000 cwt.

of

Large quantities of Paper-materials are loft in Germany, becaufe the coffins in which they lay the deceafed
are filled in the moft part of Germany with Paper-
fhavings; the bodies are likewife clothed with a linen
fhift or fhirt, and are laid on a linen fheet.

Confifcated books are burnt in Germany.

of rags, and make principally dark purple paper for the fugar-bakers The annual increafe of printing preffes, and the want of rags and Paper-ftuff, has engaged the Paper-makers to make many more reams of Paper from one cwt. of rags than formerly, which renders the prefent German printing-paper very difagreeable to the printers and readers.

There are in the kingdom of Sweden no more than 24 Paper-mills. In Stockholm alone were imported, in 1781, 18,579 reams of Paper: 8,142 reams for writing, 5,786 reams for printing, and 4,651 reams of packing-paper, and coarfer forts.

When the Czar, *Peter Alexiewitz*, vifited Drefden, in the year 1712, he faw the Paper-mill belonging to Mr. Schuchart, and made a few fheets of Paper with his own hands; he was fo pleafed with an art which furprifes every perfon who vifits a Paper-mill for the firft time, that

he

he immediately engaged Paper-makers, whom he fent to Mofcow, to eftablifh Paper-mills at his own expenfe : and Mr. Pfeiffer, a German, erected, with the affiftance of a carpenter from Commothau, a very fine Paper-manufactory; to which the faid Emperor granted great privileges. At Jaroflow is now a Paper-mill, with 28 engines and 70 vats, which manufactures weekly 1,100 reams of Paper, and confumes annually 800 tons of rags; and another which works 13 vats by 13 engines: they chiefly make Paper for Paper-hangings, which they fell at Mofcow. There are 23 Paper-mills in the Ruffian empire, and, notwithftanding they are not in want of rags (the exportation of which is prohibited), they import annually Paper to the amount of 220,000 rubles. *

In

---

* The duty to be paid on imported Paper is as follows: for writing-paper, from 2 to 5 rubles per ream; coloured Paper from 2 to 4 rubles; blotting-paper, 3 rubles; all

Paper

In the government of Kaluga are feveral
Paper-mills; and, according to Wafilii
Szujew, all offal from preparing and
weaving hemp and flax, with the fpoilt
yarn in the linen and fail-cloth manufactories, are delivered to the Paper-mills.

At the commencement of the prefent
century there were very few Paper-mills in
Holland, and the Dutch imported great
quantities of Paper till 1723 from St.
Malo, Nantz, Rochelle, and Bordeaux;
but, fince that time, they have erected
numerous mills, and carried on an extenfive
commerce, which has fuffered greatly fince
that country has been governed by the
French Republic. In the province of
Holland

Paper ufed for making cards, 3 rubles; royal, 1 ruble
60 copecs, to 2 rubles; ploughed letter-paper, in
quarto, 1 ruble 35 copecs; and if with gilt edges,
1 ruble 80 copecs; printing-paper, 75 copecs; pafte-
boards for the ufe of manufactures, 60 copecs for a
hundred.

Holland were, in 1770, eleven large and confiderable Paper-mills. In Gelderland are a great many, but fome fo fmall that they are only able to make 400 reams of Paper annually : and there are alfo water-mills with ftampers, like thofe in Germany. But in the province of Holland there are wind-mills, with cutting and grinding en-gines, which do more in two hours than the others in twelve. In Saardam, a thoufand perfons are employed in Paper-making. Holland produces not one tenth of the quantity of rags ufed in that country for Paper-manufacturing, which are fmuggled in from France, and imported from Ger-many, Italy, and Portugal ; the latter of which are of the coarfeft kind. The Dutch are chiefly jealous with refpect to this ma-nufacture, and the exportation of moulds is prohibited under pain of death. They export large quantities of Paper, principally dark purple, to Hamburgh. From 20 to 30,000 reams are annually exported to

Sweden ;

Sweden; and the exportation to France, England, Denmark, and Ruſſia, is not inconſiderable, becauſe they manufacture ſome ſorts ſuperior to thoſe manufactured in other countries.

I conclude by obſerving, that they chiefly manufacture writing-paper, and Paper of a dark purple colour, for packing ſugar-loaves. For their own printing-preſſes, they purchaſe Paper from France and Germany.

We are obliged to Mr. Meerman's indefatigable perſeverance for knowing that in 1308 linen Paper was uſed: the diſcovery of this invention may have been made ſome years ſooner, but the preciſe period cannot be poſitively aſcertained; nor in what country this invention originated.

In Italy is preſerved linen Paper, of
1367,

1367, and in Spain, of the fame year;
in England, of 1342; in France, of 1314;
and in Germany, of 1308 ; it is therefore
likely, that Germany has the honour of its
invention.

Ducarell ftates in his letter to Mr. Meerman, that, in England, many documents
from the year 1282 to 1347 are preferved;
but he acknowledges that it is impoffible to
afcertain, whether thefe manufcripts are
written on Paper made from linen, without
any mixture of cotton. Prideaux quotes a
regifter of acts from John Cranden, of the
14th year of the reign of Queen Elizabeth,
written on linen Paper in 1320 ; but it has
been determined, that, in many inftances,
he had not a competent judgment to afcertain the true quality. Mr. Aftle, who
wanted neither knowledge, nor the opportunity of making more effectual inquiries,
is filent as to the time when the linen Paper
came into ufe in England; all that he
remarks

remarks is merely a repetition of what Prideaux has ftated. There is in the library at
Canterbury, according to the Philofophical
Tranfactions of the year 1703 (No. 288,
page 515), an inventory written on linen
Paper, fpecifying the inheritance of Henry,
who was prior of Chrift-Church, and died in
1340. Dr. Wendeborn ftates, that, in the
Britifh Mufeum, there are pieces of linen
Paper from the Cottonian library, written
in the reign of Edward III. in 1342; and
he believes that if the manufcripts which it
poffeffes were carefully examined, there
might be found others of a more ancient
date.

As nothing farther has yet been afcertained, or come to public knowledge, we
muft take thefe manufcripts of 1342 for
the oldeft proof of the period when linen
Paper came into ufe in England.

The art of manufacturing Paper from
                                        linen

linen and linen-rags was only eſtabliſhed in England in the latter part of the 16th century. All Paper uſed before that time was imported from Holland and France, and ſhe paid, ſo lately as the year 1663, 100,000*l*. to the latter country, for imported Paper. A German, of the name of *Spielman*, had the happineſs, under the reign of Queen Elizabeth in 1588, to erect at Dartford, in Kent, the firſt Paper-mill; for which he received from her Majeſty the honour of Knighthood.

It is recorded in the Craftſman, No. 910, that King William III. granted the Huguenots from France, refuged in England, (Biſcoc and others,) a patent for eſtabliſhing Paper-manufactories; and parliament granted to them other privileges: but, from a want of unrelaxed perſeverance, œconomy, and induſtry, their undertaking met with the fate that often attends new eſtabliſhments: it went to ruin, notwithſtanding

ing its fuccefs in the firft few years; and
the manufacture of Paper in general de-
cayed, until the year 1713, when Thomas
Watkin, a ftationer in London, brought it
in a fhort time into great repute and perfection; and it is a merit attributable to
him, that the prefervation of this important,
moft ufeful, and neceffary of all arts has
given rife to the eftablifhment of the
numerous Paper-mills that England now
poffeffes, which manufacture very large
quantities of Paper of all forts in the
greateft perfection: not only a great part of
which is exported to foreign countries, but
the importation of this commodity is now
confined to a few affortments only, of which
there cannot be a doubt, that thefe kinds of
Paper yet imported, will foon be manufactured in this country of an equal quality,
becaufe, by perfeverance, convenience in
the conftruction of thefe manufactures,
fuperior engines, preffes and machines,
and improved moulds, the induftrious

manu-

manufacturers have been affifted and enabled to give to Englifh Paper its actual pre-
eminence.

Ireland has, during many years, offered
and paid premiums to encourage thofe
concerned in Paper-making, for the manufacture of the beft and the largeft quantities
of Paper; but notwithftanding fuch incitement, and that provifions and labour are
there cheaper than in England, it is under
the neceffity of importing confiderable
quantities from hence, and paying a higher
price than for their home-manufactured
Paper.

Scotland manufactures good printing-
paper, which greatly furpaffes that of the
Germans in whitenefs and ftrength.—
Meffrs. Foulis, printers at Glafgow, are
faid to export annually on an average
two millions of copies of books, and it
muft be prefumed that they are partly indebted

debted to the fuperiority of the Scotch
Paper, to that of Germany and the
Northern countries, for the pre-eminence
to which their printing-houfe has been
raifed..

England, which does not furnifh fuch
confiderable quantities of rags as might
have been expected from the number of
its inhabitants, and their fuperior cleanli-
nefs in linen, notwithftanding, confumes
at prefent, in its extenfive and numerous
Paper-mills, as many rags as any other
country in Europe, Germany and France
excepted. The revenue arifing from
the excife-duty on Paper amounted, in
1799, to 140,000 l. If we now calculate
that fix-fifteenth parts of the whole
quantity of Paper made in England
is writing and printing Paper, which pays
$2\frac{1}{2}d$. per pound excife-duty;* that five-
fifteenths

* Since the above was written, the duty on Paper
has been doubled, and commenced in April 1801.

fifteenths are of the fecond clafs of Paper,
paying 1 *d.* per pound; and that, of the
remaining four-fifteenth parts, one-half pays
a halfpenny per pound, and the other half
nothing; we find that 24,000,000 pounds
weight of rags and other Paper-ftuff is annually manufactured into Paper.*

One reafon that may be affigned is, that
they are not fo carefully gathered as in
other countries; but another and more
powerful one is, that the greateft part of
the English families are able to live more
comfortably than the people of other countries, and think the faving of rags not worth
their notice, or think them of fo trifling a
value, that a great part is burnt or deftroyed.
But, as I have before ftated, that the Britifh
nation is in part indebted for their wealth,
and pre-eminence above all other nations,
to the manufacture of Paper, and the art
of

* The importation of rags from the continent, in
1799, was 6,307,117 *lb.*

of printing, writing, and drawing; and as
it is certain, that the quantity of Paper
manufactured in England is the next to that
of wool, cotton, and linen, and employs not
only many thousands of hands in the mills,
but gives bread to ſtationers, authors, printers, bookſellers, and bookbinders, which
are ſo numerous with their dependents, that
it may be taken for granted, that this manufacture gives livelihood to a greater number of perſons than any other; every head
of a family ſhould therefore consider this
branch of commerce and revenue as a national concern, and follow the example of
the Dutch families, who lay by all old rags
clean waſhed, and ſell them aſſorted annually to the agents of the Paper-mills: and
there can be no doubt but the ſaving of rags
and waſte Paper in England would equally
contribute to the advantage of this valuable
manufacture.

By the act of parliament, which prohibits,
under

under a penalty, the burial of the dead in
any other drefs than wool, may be faved
about 250,000 pounds weight of linen annually *; which in other countries perifh in
the grave: but this is of little confequence
relative to the great consumption of rags,
and does not form more than one hun-
dredth part.

The want of this article obliges us therefore to import the quantity required for our
mills from abroad, until other fubftitutes
can be converted to anfwer the purpofe of
rags: till thofe are brought to perfection
and generally adopted: and until the Paper
manufactured thereof is univerfally protected, by every well-wifher to his country.
The value of the Paper manufactured in
1784 in England has been ftated to amount
to 800,000 _l._ and it will not be over-rated

Q   if

---

* Calculating that out of thirty perfons living, on the
average, one dies annually, and that one pound weight of
linen might be ufed at every burial, and the number of
inhabitants feven millions and a half.

if we give the prefent annual value, by reafon of the increafe of the ufe of Paper and
of its price, at one million and a half fter-
ling; which, after it has gone through the
hands of the ftationers, and is finifhed by
the authors, artifts, engravers, printers, and
bookbinders, and put up for fale by the
book and print-fellers and ftationers receives
fuch additional value, that its amount may
be eftimated at fome millions more.

Parliament has therefore, for the fupport
of this manufacture enacted, that rags, old
nets, and ropes (which are ufed for manufacturing pafte-boards, wrappers, and packing-paper), can be imported duty free; and
laft feffion, it likewife allowed the free importation of all wafte-paper, provided it is
torn into pieces fo that it cannot be ufed
otherwife than for being re-manufactured.
Thefe meafures will in fome degree affift the
Manufacture recently eftablifhed for that
purpofe; but notwithftanding cannot fufficiently

ciently obviate the lamentable fcarcity, and
greatly reduce the price of rags and other
paper-ftuff: the confumption of the Paper
manufactured of the latter materials (old
nets and ropes) has likewife increafed very
much, and muft be the more confiderable as
the commerce of this country is extended.

Thefe circumftances, and the eftablifhment of the *Regenerating-Paper-Manufac-
ture*,* brought to my recollection what
Bruyfet, Levier de Lifle, Fonde, Gleditch,
Greaves, Guetard, Klaproth, Linnæus, Clarus
Mayer, Reaumur, Schäffer, Seba, Stakel,
Strange, and other fcientific men had noticed, and their ideas on fubftitutes for paper-
materials. Thefe authors have ftated, that
as cotton, flax, and hemp, are the origin of
paper

---

* The re-manufacturing of Paper has been long prac-
tifed by the Chinefe; and there is, in one of the fuburbs
of Pekin, a confiderable Paper-manufacture for that purpofe, which gives employ to numerous perfons who
collect wafte-paper, which is purchafed at a low price.

and rags, other vegetables of a tender and pliable nature might probably be converted into a mucilaginous pulp, and adopted as a substitute for rags in the manufacture of Paper; and farther, that thofe vegetables that are of a brittle and harfh nature, but which can be obtained in large quantities and at moderate prices, might by art and perfeverance be made tender, without deftroying that quality which is neceffary to be retained in paper-ftuff. It is a grand *defideratum*, that thefe fuggeftions fhould be brought into effect; and it is furprizing that the obfervations of the authors above quoted fhould not have been earlier attended to by fcientific men, or rather by intelligent Papermakers, who had the road thus opened to them for their inveftigation : for, fhould any man have difcovered a commodity, which could be cheaply and plentifully fupplied in this country, as a fubftitute for rags, &c. to mould unexceptionable Paper, fuch a man would amply merit the approbation and

encou-

encouragement of the public, notwithftanding *the jealoufy* of thofe, who are acquainted
with, and followed the hints of the above-
mentioned authors, but failed in the fame
purfuit.*

Dr. Schäffer, it is true, worked with perfeverance, induftry, and ardour, to prove
that numerous vegetables were qualified to
make Paper, and his fame will be immorta-
lized;

---

* Many hints have been given by others, and principally by an ingenious literary gentleman, long refident
in India, to J. Sewell, of Cornhill, on the ufefulnefs of
many Eaft-India plants, not only for making Paper, but
likewife for the manufacture of linen cloth, fail cloth,
and cordage; but they have not yet been attended to,
notwithftanding Mr. Sewell has neither fpared expenfe
nor trouble to propagate thefe hints. Shall now a perfon
who purfues fuch hints, and is by perfeverance fuccefsful,
in making ufelefs articles valuable in manufactures and
commerce, for the benefit of his country, not be entitled to merit, and the fupport of the publick, becaufe
the firft idea has been communicated to him by others?
Linen cloth has been manufactured from flax during
feveral centuries, before the art of making fine lace of
the fame fubftance has been difcovered : this improvement was neverthelefs confidered as a new invention.

lized; but, notwithftanding that this author theorized on the fubject with great ability, he accomplifhed nothing fatisfactory by his experiments, which only tended to prove that various vegetables could probably be fo mollified as to make ufeful Paper with the addition of a fmall quantity of rags: neither himfelf, nor any perfon who has followed him, has ever been able to make it at all without rags, or, even by mixture, fit for printing, writing, paper-hanging, and other purpofes: it has only been fit for packing paper, and always brittle.

Travellers affirm that the Chinefe and Japanefe ufe a lye in their Paper-manufactories, by which they convert plants, the bark of trees, and feveral other vegetables, into a pulp,* which is afterwards moulded into a large and beautiful Paper: this Paper, however, notwithftanding its apparent fmoothnefs,

---

* All Paper made in the province of Che-Kyang is manufactured from the ftraw of rice and other grain.

nefs, is very liable to break. No author has fatisfactorily defcribed the ingredients that are ufed in making this lye, or the farther procefs that vegetables muft undergo, before they are fufficiently macerated and reduced to a ftate to be formed into Paper: and all farther information has been cautioufly concealed from us.

Nature, which is ever bountiful in fupplying all our wants, has not only provided us with numerous materials for making Paper, but alfo fhewn us in what manner vegetable fubftances may be formed into Paper, by the operation of Nature itfelf, of which G. A. Senger at Reck has given us knowledge in his *Moft Ancient Record of the Fabrication of Paper, difcovered in Nature.* It is the plant which has received the name of *conferva* from Linnæus and other naturalifts who followed Pliny; which is to be found plentifully on the top of the water in brooks, rivulets, ponds, ditches, &c.

Men

Men are little inclined to afcribe their knowledge to any other caufe than to their own inveftigation, and moft difcoveries have therefore, by manifold and exquifite improvements, obtained, by our genius, the appearance which might lead us to confider all the perfections to which arts, fciences, and manufactures are arrived, as if they had been invented and brought into exiftence entirely by ourfelves, without the aid of various accidental occurrences in the œconomy of Nature. All thefe difcoveries neverthelefs derive their origin from nothing elfe but the appearances in Nature, and men are confequently but the imitators of Nature, although in the moft laudable fenfe.

This would require a more particular and more extended inveftigation than I am willing to deliver; and an expert philofopher would only be fit for fuch an undertaking, in order to fupprefs the prejudice and felf-conceit of thofe who appropriate
their

their inventions alone to their own extended
wifdom ; and to exhibit men in their feeble-
nefs, being entirely dependent on Nature.

Nature, which lays open to every eye,
is the moft excellent fchool of all for
acquiring wifdom ; fhe forms the philofopher, and is the firft channel by which the
artift and chemift obtain knowledge and
ability ; an aftonifhing light ftreams forth
from the active ftage of Nature into our
organs, and her aim is to promote, ftep by
ftep, decency and perfection in the moral
world, if attended to, comprehended, and
properly applied. It appears, therefore,
ftrange to the ftrict obferver of the phenomena of Nature, why fo many of our arts
have not been fooner difcovered and brought
into practice.

I do not look for thefe caufes in the
myfteries wherein Nature often cloaks her
work, but rather in man himfelf, and in
his

his remiffnefs, often occafioned by circumftances, and owing to the little attention he
is accuftomed to give to her phenomena.

Many of our learned men, in order to
rectify and enlarge their ideas, confine their
diligence and obfervations only to their
books, neglecting to caft a penetrating eye
on the fecret and active operations of Nature; and a man of a fearching fpirit may
be fometimes mifled to afpire to fuperna-
tural things, and live and act in the fpecu-
lations of an imaginary fphere, and leave,
according to his imagination, the lower
regions to ideots. Nature is the beft
teacher: the information obtained from
books muft be confidered as fecondary; and
hints given to an active mind can only be
brought to perfection by combining the
inftruction received from books with thofe
which we obtain from Nature in greater
perfection. To this we muft join the incli-
nations which feem to be natural to us,
that

that we fcarcely look for things of importance in our proximity, but are rather
inclined to fearch for them at a diftance.
Thefe are undeniable grounds why many
hints for valuable difcoveries have not been
brought to perfection and practice.

Mr. Senger ftates that he became unex-
pectedly acquainted with the natural preparation and fabrication of Paper. He fays:
" In my walks on the borders of a fmall
" brook, I found both fhores on the fide
" of the hedges covered with a flimy
" fubftance, which the not long be-
" fore overflowed brook had depofited.
" The furface of the water was covered
" anew with a yellowifh green vege-
" table, and in fuch places where the
" brook had bendings, lay confiderable
" quantities of this fine vegetable produc-
" tion piled up in heaps, which gave addi-
" tional beauty to the blooming fhores of
" the flowing brook. This appearance,
                                    " and

" and the thought of an ufeful application,
" attracted me into their intereft, and de-
" termined me to examine it without de-
" lay, in order to difcover its value, becaufe
" I could not perfuade myfelf that thrifty
" Nature could have brought forth fo much
" beauty and fuch an aftonifhing great
" quantity of fleecy matter to no ufe or
" purpofe.

" This vicinity was for many days the
" place of my refort, and the little brook
" appeared to me to be a rich fountain,
" which concealed plenty of matter to in-
" creafe knowledge, which might lead to
" fome new difcoveries, and in courfe of
" time recompenfe my endeavours with
" the moft pleafing furprife.

" This covering extended on the furface
" of the water, was not only a refting-
" place for infects of various forts, and a
" well fecured ftore-houfe for their broods,

but

" but as Nature intends every where to
" give multiplicity of advantages, I ex-
" perienced very foon that it contained a
" proper ftuff for making Paper, and what
" is more furprifing, a Paper prepared
" by Nature alone, without the affiftance
" of imitating proceffes.

" This peculiar web contains innume-
" rable fleecy parts of vegetation, which
" are generated, in the firft part of the
" fpring, on ponds and other ftanding wa-
" ters; they detach themfelves from the
" bottom, and rife on the furface, where
" they appear as a handfome green and
" yellow covering. After thefe fleecy
" particles have remained for fome
" time on the watery mirror; by the
" heat of the fun, and by the changing
" degrees of cold and warmth of the wa-
" ter, they become more united and felted
" together, bleached, and at laft turned
" into a tough Paper-like covering. Or,

if

" if this fleecy fubftance is mixed together,
" and carried away by fudden inundations,
" occafioned by heavy rains, and depofited
" on the fhores, it appears then like a thin
" jelly or flime, which, after it has under-
" gone feveral changes naturally produced
" by the contents of air and water, turns
" into a kind of Paper, which refembles
" the common Paper; or, where it has
" been produced upon clean water, it is
" not unlike a fuperior Paper, of which
" fome may be gathered nearly as white
" as writing Paper."

Muft we not, with humble fubmiffion, ftill more revere the hand of the all-wife Creator in the works of Nature, when we find that fhe proceeds in this operation in the fame manner as the Paper-maker in his mill, when he attempts to prepare Paper out of rags. This fleecy fubftance rifes from the bottom of the water, and feparates from its origin and vegetation, which is the

firft

firſt procefs; thefe materials are then prepared upon the furface of the water by the
apparently invifible contents of all waters,
which are in fome more, in others lefs; by the
fofteſt of all waters, rain; by the refreſhing
air of the night; by the heat of the fun;
and by glutinous and oily fubftances. The
waves or motion of the water reduces
it into the fmalleft particles, without deftroying its texture, like a pulp made of
rags when ground in the Paper-engine.
The graffy fhore receives at laft this Paper-
ftuff manufactured by Nature alone, like
the artift, who fcoops in the Paper-mill
the prepared materials upon frames, out of
the vat, and depofits it upon hairy felts,
in order to prefs and dry it. Mr. Senger is
therefore entitled to the thanks of men,
who too often overlook the moft ingenious
works of Nature, by giving them hints to
fix their thoughts on this phenomenon,
which reprefents to us fo clearly the original fabrication of Paper, and hands down
to

to us the firſt and moſt ancient records
thereof; in the ineffectual purſuit of which
our anceſtors have ſpent many centuries,
and could never diſcover it to its full extent.
It was left to the laſt year of the 18th century, to prove to the world that a ſtrong
Paper can be manufactured from all vegetable ſubſtances, on following thoſe rays which
Nature has laid open to our eyes.

It is natural to enquire how this phœnomenon could remain ſo long hidden
from the ſearching eye of men; or, if it
was known, why did they not make uſe
thereof; and learn from it, the uſeful
art of making Paper? The more ſo, as this
phœnomenon extends itſelf over the whole
ſurface of the globe; and as a thinking
man, who poſſeſſes a ſpeculating ſpirit, with
a great mind not to relax his purſuits by
diſappointment, but to perſevere in his
undertakings, may be by it ſo eaſily led
to the diſcovery of the artificial manufacture

ture of Paper, after fo many hints have been thrown out by the before quoted authors. Have not many years expired fince Dr. Schäffer produced a Paper mixed with rags, made from a kind of vegetable which he calls *water-wool*, and which was this *Conferva*?

This river Paper is completely fabricated by Nature, fo as to be fit for writing or printing, if only taken from the furface of the water when ripe, (which is to be afcertained by taking a handful, fqueezing the water out, and finding it fibrous,) hung up and dried, and fmoothed with an iron.

It remains now to ftate which kind of *Conferva* is the moft ufeful for making Paper, and may be plentifully obtained. Linnæus fays that there are 21 forts of *Conferva*, which I mean not to difpute, but to name thofe that are the fitteft for the before-mentioned purpofe, which are: *Conferva rivularis; Conferva bullofa; Conferva reticu-*

R   *latis.*

latis. Thefe three can be gathered in abundance in fummer and autumn, the time when ripe, purified, and united by the warmth of the fun, by means of oily fubftances formed likewife in the water by Nature. Mr. Senger fays, that two children have gathered one thoufand weight in one day.

I have heretofore ftated the want felt by fociable men in the earlieft ages, to difcover means by which might be preferved to pofterity ufeful and notable occurrences of time, the progrefs of arts and fciences, and in general to facilitate traffic amongft men. Tradition, which for a feries of years was a fubftitute for writing, did but little in comparifon to this art; many things of great importance were forgotten; many valuable fciences were loft, mutilated, or but confufedly handed down to pofterity. After letters were invented, a beginning was made to give, as it were,

fpeech

fpeech to rocks and metals, and to engrave
on them memorable events. By degrees,
art facilitated this gigantic mode, and taught
to exchange this uncommon bulky manner
of writing into an eafier method, and to
tranfcribe it on tables, which were fuperfeded by metals, bones, and wood, until
fkins, barks, &c. were made ufe of. Centuries elapfed before a more convenient
material to write upon was difcovered ; and
many unfuccefsful experiments were made,
and long years of labour were given up by
the greateft men of fcience, before the difcovery of the Egyptian *Papyrus*, and the
art of making Paper from cotton and linen
rags was invented.

The linen-rag Paper, which has fo much
improved and benefited mankind, was by
degrees employed to other purpofes than
writing, and naturally very much encreafed
the price of rags, which makes the Paper
fo fcarce, that fufficient quantities cannot be

obtained

obtained for the ufe of the numerous print-
ing-offices, not only in England, but in all
other enlightened countries; and accounts
that have been received from various parts
of the Continent fhew that the price of
rags will augment rather than abate. Confiderations on thefe circumftances induced
me to make further trials, and endeavour
to accomplish that which had been thought
impoffible by others, and which had baffled
the attempts of many ingenious men, notwithftanding the road had been opened to
them by Nature, and the hints of men.
My labours and perfeverance have been
crowned with fuccefs.

I have had the fatisfaction to witnefs the
eftablifhment of an extenfive Paper-manufactory, fince the firft of May 1800, at
the Neckinger Mill, Bermondfey, where
my invention of re-manufacturing Paper
is carried on with great fuccefs, and
where there are already more than 700

reams

reams weekly manufactured, of perfectly
clean and white Paper, made without any
addition of rags, from old waste, written and
printed Paper; by which the Publick has
already been benefited so far, that the price
of Paper has not risen otherwise than by
the additional duty thereupon, and the en-
creased price of labour. And it will not
be many weeks before double that quantity
will be manufactured at the said mill.

Thus far succeeding, my other more
extended views, in assiduously endeavour-
ing to manufacture the most perfect Paper
from straw, wood, and other vegetables, have
been likewise successful. And I am able
to produce to the publick very strong and
fine Paper, made thereof, without any addition of other known Paper-stuff, notwithstanding I have not yet had the advantage
of making it in a mill, regularly built for
such a new undertaking. The Paper where-
upon

upon this is printed is an undeniable proof.*
It is however only of an inferior quality,
being made from the ftraw in the ftate it
comes from the farm yard, without afforting
the weeds, and thofe parts of the ftraw
which have been coloured by the weather.
I have ufed this kind of Paper on purpofe
to demonftrate the progrefs of fo fingular
an undertaking, and to prove its poffibility
to the world, notwithftanding the opinion
of many fcientific men, particularly that of
the ingenious Breitkopf at Leipzic, that
Paper made from ftraw cannot be ufed for
printing. This fpecimen, and others of a
much finer quality which have been manufactured, leave no doubt, that, when the
manufactory has been regularly eftablifhed
with the neceffary implements, I fhall make
ftraw Paper in as great perfection as any
made from rags ; and by feveral trials which
I have made to change the yellow colour
into cream colour, and white, it feems to be
unquef-

* Part of this edition is printed on Straw Paper.

ùnqueftionably practicable, which will extend its confumption, and remove the
prejudices which are generally cherifhed
againft new difcoveries; notwithftanding
its natural colour is not only pleafing, but
grateful to the eye for writing and printing,
principally for mufick-notes by candle-light.
Copper-plate printers affert that it takes
the impreffion fuperior to French copper-
plate paper, and it has a beautiful effect in
landfcapes and pictures, for drawing, and
paper-hangings.

In my former edition I faid, (p. 79) " I
flatter myfelf that my exertions will meet
with the approbation and fupport of the
community at large." Since which my
expectations have been gratified, not only
by the fanction of the legiflature, who have
been pleafed to pafs an act of parliament,
by which my undertaking has been greatly
facilitated, fo that I am now able to eftablifh this manufacture to a confiderable
extent.

extent, but alfo, by the approbation and
fupport of perfons of the firft refpectability,
who have come forward to patronize it;
which is the ftrongeft teft the publick can
require of its general utility, and national
importance; the laft of which is certainly of
much greater extenfion than by many is
conceived; becaufe, by the eftablifhment
of a large manufacture of this kind, numerous hands of both fexes, and of all ages,
will be employed and gain their livelihood,
who now are, or otherwife might become,
a burthen to the parifhes in which they re-
fide; it will increafe the revenue; it will
prevent the necefsity of fending large fums
of money out of this kingdom, for the purchafing of rags;* it will render feveral of
the

* If from 5,000 to 6,000 loads of ftraw will be converted annually into Paper, ufed for Paper-hangings, it
will be equal to the quantity of rags imported from the
continent in 1799. A great part of thofe rags are ufed
for that kind of Paper (elephant,) that being of a ftronger
texture than Englifh rags. And as Paper-hangings made
from

the commodities to be employed in this manufacture more valuable and useful than they have hitherto been, (many of which have been thrown away) which of courfe is interefting to the landed property of this country, as the value of land muft naturally encreafe; and it will ultimately reduce the price of Paper.

But whether or not this country can avail itfelf of all the advantages that are likely to refult from a difcovery which promifes to become fo generally ufeful, muft, in my humble opinion, intirely depend on thofe meafures, which the legiflature of this country fhall in their wifdom think it prudent to adopt, in order to prevent the difcovery from

from ftraw Paper may be manufactured much cheaper to the tafte of the people abroad, than they can make it from rags, this country will be enabled to provide the whole world with it, *at a lower rate than it is poffible to be manufactured from rags,* and foreigners will be neceffitated to fend their money to this country for the purchafe of it.

S

from being known to other countries :—a meafure not undeferving the attention of the Britifh government, at this conjuncture, when the fplendor of its manufactures and commerce is more envied than at any former period of our hiftory,

By *the fanction with which the legiflature has favoured my difcovery* ; by *the fupport of men of fortune and refpectability* who have come forward to facilitate my endeavours to eftablifh this manufacture on fuch a fcale as to make it of importance to the publick; and by *the approbation with which it has been honoured by numerous perfons*; I flatter myfelf to overcome all prejudices againft this new invented *wood, ftraw,* and *vegetable Paper,* and that I fhall, by my unremitting perfeverance, bring the difcovery to the greateft perfection, and that my efforts will render it eligible for general ufe : then the opinions and judgments, which are inconfiderately or envioufly circulated to the

injury

injury of many new inventions and eſtabliſhments, will be turned to its advantage,
and promote its proſperity, which are the
moſt effectual means, not only to prevent
a further riſe of the price of Paper, but contribute to its reduction.

It will be productive of the greateſt ſatisfaction, if, by farther reſearches, I can
accompliſh the object I have in view,
namely, that of manufacturing Paper from
vegetables, for the purpoſe of making bank-
notes, which by the experiments I have
made I am convinced I ſhall be able to
effect. A diſcovery of ſuch deſcription muſt
be a ſource of great and pleaſant reflection
to every philanthropic mind, ſince the op-
portunities of forgery on the Bank of England, which at preſent exiſt, will be moſt
effectually done away, and the publick mind
relieved from hearing of ſuch crimes, and of
the executions which enſue from the con-
viction of the offenders. That ſuch will be
the

the good confequences refulting to the community, from manufacturing Paper of the
faid materials for the before-mentioned
purpofe, muft be manifeft, becaufe the
mixture of vegetables from which the Paper
would be made might remain a fecret, if
the neceffary meafures for that purpofe are
adopted: confequently no forgery could
henceforth be committed on the Bank, as
long as fuch Paper fhould be ufed in making
bank-notes, becaufe the counterfeiting of
the Paper cannot take place, as long as
the materials from which it is made is unknown, and as long as the Patent granted by
His Majefty is in force.

APPENDIX.

APPENDIX.

As an Appendix to this little Tract, I think it proper to fubmit a few more remarks on the National Importance of difcovering materials which can be converted into Paper, and grow fufficiently abundant in Great Britain, without the neceffity of importing them from foreign countries.

The following lines are printed upon Paper made from Wood alone, the produce of this country, without any intermixture of rags, wafte paper, bark, ftraw, or any other vegetable fubftance,

T   from

from which Paper might be, or has
hitherto been manufactured; and of
this the moft ample teftimony can be
given, if neceffary.

Having thus far fucceeded in my refearches, to make an ufeful Paper
from one kind of Wood, I doubt not,
but, that I fhall find many others equally
eligible for the fame purpofe, of which
I truft it will be in my power, within
a few weeks, to give indifputable
proof that my expectations have been
well founded, and that I have not
cherifhed a vifionary opinion.

Hiftory furnifhes us with numerous
examples of one difcovery giving birth
to others, and, if my fuccefs of having encreafed the quantity of Paper
materials, by rendering thefe applica-
ble to that which have never been
before applied to fuch a purpofe,
fhould

fhould incite active and induftrious
artifts, to make farther improvements in
their various manufactures, my feelings
will be amply gratified. Various hints
may be fuggefted to thofe who are
already acquainted with the properties
of Paper, when pafted in lamina on
each other; it may, by this means,
be made to form a fubftance, as durable and more impenetrable than oak.

Having long admired the celebrated
manufacture of Mr. *Clay*, at Birming-
ham, who has demonftrated to what perfection and beauty it has been brought,
it will, in the courfe of time, perhaps
not be furprifing to find, that objects
of greater confequence will engage
their attention in the fame purfuit,
and prove, that the properties from
fucceffive layers of Paper, may be
found a fubftitute for many purpofes,

for

for which at prefent foreign Wood is required.

One of the greateft obftacles to the improvement and extenfion of this art has been probably the fcarcity of the raw materials. Now that thefe are found *at home* in fufficient abundance, means may be found to fupply manufactures with any quantity required, at reduced prices.

It may probably be ultimately proved, that Paper thus prepared, will be a lighter, neater, and more durable covering for buildings of all kinds, and it is equally true, that the ingredients, with which the cement can be compofed, will render this fubftance not only incombuftible, bnt more durable than flates, tiles, (which in the courfe of time become brittle) and wood in

it

its natural ftate, and incorruptible by infects. Who can fay that coach-makers, chair-makers, and cabinet-makers, will not make ufe of it for carriages, chairs, and elegant houfehold furniture, and reflect that a fubftance poffeffing fuch fuperior properties ought to be preferred; having flexibility, hardnefs, and capability of being worked with infinite greater neatnefs and luftre than wood, which is fo much affected by the air and weather. Converting wood, ftraw, and other vegetable fubftances into Paper, may there-fore be rendered ufeful for a variety of purpofes; and the fubftance of the Wood Paper on which thefe lines are printed, (which is the firft attempt to make it in a quantity) exhibits an indifputable proof, that ufeful Paper may be manufactured from the hardeft part of wood alone, deftitute of its pith or bark; and, if

any

any of the fuggeftions here ftated, as
to the application of the manufactured
material fhould be thought reafonable,
experiments of fome able manufacturers
will prove, that this Paper can be
again converted into a fubftance, more
hard and durable than any wood of
natural growth.

Confidering, in its full extent, the
numerous ufes to which the difcovery
of making Paper from wood, ftraw and
other vegetables, which always can be
obtained in this country at moderate
prices, can be applied, it is certainly
an invention that merits attention
and fupport. If only fit for the manufacture of inferior forts of Paper,
and Paper-hangings, this country will
be enabled to cope with the whole
world in this fpecies of commerce, on
the moft advantageous terms, and to
enrich

enrich herfelf, by opening this new fource of trade, very lucrative to the revenue, and allowing the manufactured commodity to be fold for lefs than the prefent price of Paper; whilft, at the fame time, it will make feveral materials * more valuable, and, by giving employment to thoufands of women and children, thereby eftablifh an influx of real wealth into this country.

The wifdom of the legiflature has rendered it neceffary that the fpecification of every patent fhould be made public within the fpace of twenty-eight days, which has been fometimes extended to fix months. The patentee's benefit exifts for fourteen years, and is extremely well protected by the law againft the infringement of its privileges, by the inhabitants of Great Britain; but it appears very extraordinary, that
every

* Saw-duft, wood-fhavings, old mattings, &c.

every patent is open for the infpection
of foreigners, and that the patentee
remains unprotected with refpect to
them. A pamphlet has been fuffered
to be publifhed monthly, fince the
year 1794, which defcribes not only
the exifting patents of the country,
but contains complete drawings and
defcriptions of new-invented machines. This pamphlet has been, and
will be, immediately tranflated into
the continental languages; a practice
which has, no doubt, proved highly
detrimental to the revenue and com=
mercial intereft of this country.

If a patent is obtained for an ingenious invention, which may have coft
the author many years intenfe labour
and ftudy, and the refult produces
great national wealth by the manufacture and exportation of the commodity, the profpects may be clouded in

an

an hour, and all expectation baffled
by foreigners reading the fpecification,
who, by erecting fimilar manufactures
abroad, under greater advantages,*
deprive the country of the revenue
and commerce. If this fubject was
duly weighed, it furely might be
remedied. It may be afked, why a
patent is to be openly exemplified before its term is expired? for, as it can
be of no ufe to the inhabitants of
this country, during the fpace of fourteen years, for what purpofe is it expofed? and why are foreigners permitted to reap the benefits to which
this country is only entitled? It is
undeniable, that it operates as a per-
petual difcouragement to the future
efforts of genius, preventing monied
men from carrying the moft valuable dif-

v   coveries

---

* They do not want to fpend money to bring the invention to perfection; and manual labour, building, and rent is
cheaper on the Continent.

coveries into effect. The doubtfulnefs
of fuccefs alone fufficiently damps the
ardour, perfeverance, and exertions
neceffarily required in the purfuit of
fkilful and laborious inquiries; but,
having fucceeded to his utmoft wifhes
and after having incurred very injuri-
ous expenfes in the profecution of
his defign, he is foiled in all his hopes
of compenfation, by the expofure of
the means through which the difcovery has been effected. This confideration alone ought to weigh with
thofe by whom this evil can be remedied to the individual. But, much
as it may be lamented, this injury
bears no proportion to the loffes which
the revenue and commerce fuffer.

It therefore appears impolitic in the
laft degree to expofe the exemplification of a patent to public difclofure,
and to be a *defideratum* of fuch infinite

finite importance, that the Legiflature may think of fome method to prevent the art from being divulged in a patent, and being purloined by foreigners, who are jealous of the greatnefs of the manufactures, commerce, and navigation, of Great Britain.

The importance of this is fufficiently obvious by daily experience; and it feems very aftonifhing that the Legiflature has not before taken it up as a general meafure; as it is not only a great hardfhip, but an act of injuftice, that the people of this country fhould be reftrained from the ufe of inventions, for which patents have been granted, for a term of fourteen years, which foreigners can immediately avail themfelves of abroad, by procuring copies of the fpecifications inrolled here, which it is notorious they are in the daily habit of doing, and which ftands proved in the Report of

v 2   laft

laft Seffions of Parliament by the Committee, to be confidered by them as a
matter of great importance, from their
remitting money to Bankers in this kingdom to pay perfons for collecting and
fending over particulars of our Difcoveries
and Manufactures. One cannot help obferving the impolicy of that legiflative
act, which declares it a crime for any fubject or other perfon in this realm to fend
abroad any machine or other apparatus
ufed in our manufactures: yet permits
written and printed copies of the particulars of inventions, and prints of machinery, to be daily tranfmitted abroad: nay,
fuffers a work monthly to be publifhed
in this metropolis, avowing itfelf to be
a defcription of inventions and difcoveries, and the mode in which they
are effected, together with the plates
of all the machinery, which publication
is tranflated abroad in different languages. Is it to be contended that a
fkilful

ſkilful mechanic cannot make a machine
from a drawing and complete deſcription of machinery, but only from the actual machine itſelf?   The only objection
that ſeems to oppoſe itſelf to this meaſure is, that it would be a hardſhip
to puniſh a man for an infringement
of an invention, the mode of carrying
on which, he has not an opportunity
of inſpecting before committing the act,
and therefore could not intentionally have
infringed, but of which he would have
had the previous inſpection, if the ſpe-
cification was inrolled as directed.   The
anſwer to which is, that particular and
private inconvenience ought to give way
to general good; but here, (by my
patent) that ſacrifice is not required to
be made, and I think there will not any
real inconvenience be ſuſtained by this
meaſure being generally adopted for all
patents which may be granted.

My

My patent being for making Paper from Straw, &c. during the term of fourteen years; no perfon has any right during that period to make it from fuch raw materials as are defcribed in my patent; and I have proved to the Committee of both Houfes of Parliament by fatisfactory evidence, that the perfect Paper exhibited there was made folely from the fubftances mentioned in the patent: but, fuppofing a perfon to have difcovered a new mode of making Paper from Straw, much more ufeful and beneficial than the prefent, and that it was neceffary he fhould fee the exemplification of mine, to fhew that his is original, and not an infringement on my invention, he has only to apply to the Lord High-Chancellor, whom I humbly fubmit fhould have the control over the keepers of my exemplification, and on verifying the facts, he would immediately direct an infpection. I truft the Legiflature

Legiſlature will not eſteem unworthy of their notice my obſervation for the benefit of the country, revenue and commerce.

FINIS.

For EU product safety concerns, contact us at Calle de José Abascal, 56–1°,
28003 Madrid, Spain or eugpsr@cambridge.org.